PEOPLE AND PARLIAMENT

PEOPLE
AND
PARLIAMENT

Nigel Nicolson

WEIDENFELD AND NICOLSON
7 CORK STREET LONDON WI

© 1958 by Nigel Nicolson

PRINTED IN GREAT BRITAIN

SET IN 11 POINT GARAMOND
BY EBENEZER BAYLIS AND SON LTD., THE
TRINITY PRESS, WORCESTER, AND LONDON
N. 6381

CONTENTS

To

PHILIPPA

ὀλίγη δόσις ἀλλ' ἀπὸ θυμοῦ

ACKNOWLEDGMENTS

The authors and publishers have kindly allowed me to quote from the following works: *Official Report* (*Hansard*) of the House of Commons and House of Lords debates (H.M. Stationery Office). *British Political Parties* by R. T. McKenzie (Heinemann). *The Electoral System in Britain 1918–51* by D. E. Butler (Clarendon Press). *Elections and Electors* by J. F. S. Ross (Eyre and Spottiswoode). *Government and Parliament* by Herbert Morrison (Oxford University Press). *The Labour Party in Perspective* by C. R. Attlee (Gollancz). *How People Vote* by Mark Benney, A. P. Gray and R. H. Pear (Routledge and Kegan Paul).

PREFACE

THIS book would probably never have been written if I had not become involved in an unhappy dispute with some of my constituents. It is partly addressed to them. But its main purpose is to discuss the general principles which our controversy has raised.

There is uncertainty in the public's mind, and to a lesser extent in Parliament, about the duty of an elected representative when he finds himself in disagreement with his political party and with those who elected him. Some say that an educated people with universal suffrage have a right to greater control over their Member of Parliament than is suggested by the familiar distinction between a representative and a delegate. Others say that the principles which Burke so brilliantly enunciated nearly two hundred years ago have become even truer today. I believe the latter view to be correct. I see as much danger as advantage in a Member's subservience to his party. For a time it may be a convenience, and an aid to steady government. In the end it can only lead to the impotence of Parliament itself.

I have illustrated this theme by three actual examples: the dispute over capital punishment; the Suez crisis of 1956; and the events in my own constituency. My purpose is to reconsider these controversies calmly and from a certain distance, and to discover whether they hold any lessons of value to our democracy.

N.N.

Shirley House, Bransgore, Christchurch
June 1958

1*

Chapter One

REPRESENTATION
AND MISREPRESENTATION

Success of British democracy—function of Parliament—function of a repre-
sentative—Council of Europe compared to the States of Alderney—direct
representation is impossible—function of political parties—evils of the party
system—the charade of politics—elimination of the independent Member—
erosion of independence—likely effects of increased party discipline—the extent
of party pressure on Members today—theory versus practice

IN 1914 DICEY suggested that only by the 1950s should we be
in a position to judge whether British democracy had succeeded or
not. The franchise had been greatly extended during his own life-
time and he wondered whether so large a number of politically
uneducated electors (soon, though he could not know it, to be
doubled by the admission of women to the vote) would not en-
slave their representatives and make orderly government impossible. His question could have been broadly answered long before
the 1950s. Owing to a remarkable combination of restraint on the
part of the electorate, and of tact, vigour and innocent deceit on
the part of their leaders, British democracy has hitherto emerged
successful from its most important test: unpopular decisions by a
Government are, in general, accepted; and popular clamour weighs
no more than an ounce or two in the scales of its judgement.

But Dicey's question can never be finally answered. Democracy
cannot be said to have succeeded because it has won two wars,
since the process of winning them involved the suspension of
many of its attributes and forms. Nor can its success be measured
by the degree of power and influence which the country exerts in
the world. It is simple to imagine a theoretically perfect democracy
stage-managing a nation's steady decline. If, fifty years hence,
Britain has become, on the scale of the modern world, the equivalent of Athens in the fourth century BC, it will not be democracy
which will have failed her; but a misuse of the weapons of democracy may have contributed to her weakening. Nothing is easier
than inadvertently to turn their sharp edges against ourselves. So
in each decade, the question is worth reframing: is the British

democratic system falling out of balance? At the present moment, the precise form of the question might be: Is the shift of power from Parliament to the executive, and from Parliament to the great party organizations outside, distorting the system to such an extent that Parliament itself is in danger of being crushed?

It might be argued that no great harm would be done if Parliament became no more than a transforming-station between the people and the executive. If it is the essence of democratic government, as Asquith defined it, 'that the will of the people shall, both in legislation and policy, prevail', it could be made to appear admirable that modern techniques such as television and the mass party conferences should bring the rulers into direct touch with the ruled, without the intervention of an elected body which might hamper the activities of one and distort the opinions of the other. Not many would be prepared to sustain such an argument, if only because Parliament is composed of men and women professionally equipped to digest an enormous variety of facts and opinions fed to them from above and below, from Ministers and from their constituents, and no alimentary canal can be a substitute for a stomach. Still the theory grows in strength that the Member of Parliament, if his party is in power, is no more than an interpreter of his supporters' opinions, and an exponent of the Government's decisions based upon them: and that, if he is in opposition, his interpreter's role is the same, but his duty is to make out the worst possible case for the Government's actions. No Member would define his function in this way, but pressure is being put upon him to accept it if he wishes to retain his seat. A Parliament composed exclusively of men who came to think of themselves in this role would no longer be a Parliament capable of rising to a sudden national emergency or of introducing more than purely partisan legislation.

The new interpretation has crept in under the most respectable colours, in the name of democracy itself. The second war, unlike the first, was fought to preserve the democratic way of life. The emotional climate of the war was extended at both ends, before the fighting started and after it stopped. We were inflamed in the 'thirties by Hitler's treatment of his political opponents; and we are militantly convinced today of the superiority of the democratic

system over Communism. For twenty-five years it has been axio-
matic that the test between right and wrong in a constitution is
the degree to which the ordinary man has the right to protest,
and the power to make his protest effective. Hence any innova-
tion, any disturbance of the existing balance, which increases his
control over those who rule him, is assumed to be a further step
away from everything which we most dislike, and therefore in
itself desirable.

Politicians inadvertently encouraged this notion. The Labour
Government, by enormously expanding the scope of the welfare
services, suggested to the voter that hitherto his true needs and
deserts had been disregarded by his representatives, whose main
duty now was to attend to his wishes. The Conservatives, by
making freedom the battle-cry of four successive election campaigns, encouraged him to demand relief from often imaginary or
very necessary shackles of government. The great reversals of the
General Elections of 1945 and 1950–51 gave the electorate a new
sense of their tremendous latent strength. Recurrent proof of the
throttling power of the Trades Unions and the Civil Service drew
away from Parliament much of its authority. Its periodic and
largely irrelevant attempts to re-establish it by asserting its ancient
privileges, usually brought more ridicule on its head than honour.
At the same time, membership of Parliament declined in prestige.
The Member was increasingly lampooned in caricature and on the
music-hall stage as a figure of ludicrous self-importance. He was
seen not only to be paid, but to protest publicly and ignominiously
that his pay was not enough. Outstanding young men were no
longer entering Parliament, and the gap left by University members was not filled by men who had made their careers and reputations outside. It is not surprising that the electors, even without
the stimulus of mounting party warfare, should have begun to
think less and less of the status and opinions of the average back-
bench Member, and to demand of him as the price of his seat an
obedience which would have shocked their grandfathers.

Their grandfathers were usually satisfied by the tag, 'Your
Member is your representative, but not your delegate,' without
bothering much about its implications. But today the notion is
confused, if not actually challenged. The same person will accept

it as a proper principle at one moment, and reject it as a constitutional outrage at the next. 'Of course,' he will say in the
generous mood induced by the success of his candidate at the
polls, 'of course I shall not expect you automatically to adopt my
opinions as your own, even if it means that you sometimes step
outside the party line. We are sending you to Westminster to
speak and vote for us as you think best in the light of the arguments you hear and of the detailed information which we cannot
hope to have.' But when the honeymoon is over, and an issue
arises in Parliament on which the Member takes a view greatly
different from that of the majority of those who sent him there,
the tune is liable to change rapidly, and the new argument can
sound even more convincing than the first. 'We sent you to be
our representative,' the supporter now says. 'You know what the
great majority of us feel about this business. And yet you
deliberately do the opposite. What on earth is the meaning of
representation if you defy the known wishes of your supporters?'

If Parliament had no executive powers, or if the electorate were
so small that the people could make their wishes known directly,
the question could not even arise. In the first case, few would care
what opinions were expressed, for nobody's life or livelihood
could be affected by them. In the second case, it would be indis-
putable that democracy had no meaning if the authorities did one
thing when the people had unmistakably indicated that they all,
or nearly all, desired the opposite. It might be objected that no
such Parliaments exist. They do. I have recently been a member
of one of the first type, and watched one of the second type in
action.

The Assembly of the Council of Europe has no executive
powers. It only has power of recommendation to a Committee of
Ministers, who turn down with increasing politeness one resolution after another submitted to them from below. The Ministers
are rarely even present in the debating chamber. They hear none
of the arguments; they only read the formal conclusions. They are
not subject to questioning, and they are under no obligation to
account for their rejection of the Assembly's wishes. For the
representatives gathered together at Strasbourg from sixteen
European parliaments, the experience is at first exhilarating, but

after two or three sessions, profoundly depressing. It is exhilarating because of the novelty of addressing a Parliament with no
front bench to monopolize hours of debating time or to build
chinkless walls of argument around unalterable Cabinet decisions.
The resolutions can at least be voted with acclamation and sent
defiantly upstairs. But ineffectiveness gradually saps vitality, and
the visiting Member finds it increasingly difficult to justify to himself and to his constituents his absence and his expense account.
Three years at Strasbourg taught me that a Parliament without
power, an Assembly which is non-representative and consultative
only in name, is tame compared to the dangerous responsibilities
of Westminster.

At the opposite extreme lie the States of the Isle of Alderney.
A few years ago, the States allowed a prominent resident to take
in a few acres of rock and foreshore to add to his garden. The
ground was useless for any other purpose, but it happened to
form part of the common land. The islanders rose in fury. Overnight, posters appeared on the walls of the small town of St.
Anne's, lampoons in outraged doggerel were thrust through the
letter boxes of the Members of the States who had allowed this
thing to happen, and the terraces which the innocent gardener
had begun to construct were levelled with bulldozers and choked
with rocks and refuse. A People's Meeting was called, which the
entire adult population of 450 were eligible to attend. They passed
a resolution which was unanimous and unanswerable. The
decision was revoked. The terraces were swept away. The
islanders went back to their cabbages and cattle, and at the succeeding election returned all the sitting Statesmen with increased
majorities. They had been taught their lesson.

The ideal parliament would combine the abstractions of Strasbourg with the Aristotelian methods of Alderney. An elected *élite*
would debate, turning every issue inside out for public inspection;
the people would decide. But the ideal is impossible. The compromise for a large democratic and sovereign community such as
our own, is representative government, a Parliament elected
periodically by universal suffrage, and a Cabinet to direct its
debates and supply a lead.

If the ideal is impossible, it could be said, surely we must approximate to it as closely as we can? If the people cannot vote for themselves, their representatives must vote for them, and a representative is good or bad according to the fidelity with which he reproduces his electors' views in the speeches he makes and the votes he casts. Just because fifty million people are unmanageable as a committee, the 630 men and women chosen by them have no right to come to conclusions different from those which the fifty million would have reached had it been possible to assemble them all in a single place. The Member, A, can only claim to represent the electors, B, C and D, if he acts as B, C and D would act if they had the time and opportunity to do so.

This argument, so attractive and apparently final, ignores the complicating factors of practical politics. First, B, C and D are most unlikely to come to identical conclusions on every subject, and A, sooner or later, will be forced to adopt one of their differing views and so risk offending two out of his three electors. Secondly, A, who has far more opportunity to discover the facts and weigh the arguments, may decide that B, C and D are all wrong, either in the end they desire or in the means by which they imagine that it can be attained. Or the ends and means may be irreconcilable. The electors might, for instance, object to heavy taxation, while demanding the benefits which only heavy taxation can bring. Thirdly, B, C and D can seldom define what they do want beyond expressing the vaguest desire for universal peace and prosperity, and A will soon discover that his main function is not to repeat the ideas put into his mind by his electors, nor even to disentangle them, but to suggest them. Finally, A himself is a person, with prejudices and private interests, conscience and ambition, and it would be impossible, even if he willed it, for him to place these private motives in a separate compartment of his mind. Direct representation for all these reasons is a fantasy, even in the absence of a party system.

The party system does, in fact, bring it a little nearer realization. It reduces multiple points of view to two or three, and so makes opinion inside and outside Parliament more manageable. It organizes A's mind as well as the minds of his electors. A political party fuses minor differences to the point where they can be ignored, and gives guidance on major issues of policy in such a way that guidance is usually indistinguishable from decision. The party followers are unaware of the extent to which their beliefs are in fact ideas which they have accepted from above. There is nothing more likely to embed an opinion deeply in a man's mind than the suggestion that he thought of it first.

A party makes vague aspirations articulate and effective. In this sense its function is so valuable, so irreplaceable, that it is almost impossible to conceive of a democratic society without it. Opposing me at a by-election in 1952 was an Independent candidate whose declared purpose was to disrupt the party system, to which he attributed many of the evils of the day. How did he set about it? By forming a party of his own, by organizing a canvass, by displaying his slogans and colours all over the town, by raking his supporters into committee rooms; by adopting, in fact, the very methods against which he claimed to be protesting. No doubt, if other candidates had been persuaded to stand for the same beliefs in other constituencies, he would soon have found himself appointed leader, set up a Central Office and research department, and as leader he would have fought against any heresies which arose in his ranks.

To an extent, however, his protest was justified. There are evils in the party system which may be unavoidable, but which should be exposed from time to time in case we are trapped into thinking of them as merits. The first is the gulf which may be opened between leaders and led by the process of simplifying and dramatizing complicated issues. A platform speech will not raise the temperature of a meeting nor the reputation of the speaker if it is interlarded with the qualifications which he would undoubtedly make in the privacy of his office. If, for example, the theme of a series of Ministerial speeches is the greatness of our country, it may lead to a demand that our greatness be demonstrated in ways which the Ministers had never intended and cannot satisfy. If an important speech dwells on the hardships of old age, it is not surprising if the pensioners begin to think of themselves as victims of an injustice, when the injustice, if it exists at all, is one which no Government has the financial resources to remedy. Politicians have nobody to blame for this dilemma but themselves. They have taught the public that parties survive by battling successfully against other parties, that hard-hitting is an epithet of approval, and that reasonableness in politics is rarely sweet. A kid-glove candidate is a disappointment to his supporters because they have been led to expect a fight and not a discussion. The very terminology of politics is military and evangelical: 'campaign', 'strategy', 'tactics', 'standard-bearer'; and 'converts', 'faith', 'missionary', 'creed'. It is the language of the Crusades.

Nor is it used only on the hustings. Parliament itself is caught up in an unceasing battle with wooden swords. A logically developed argument often catches fire only when the weariest slogans of party warfare are tacked on the end, and the strophes and antistrophes of back-bench recrimination begin to fly across the Chamber. The public do not read next day of the grins that accompanied them, nor of the long hours of patient and tolerant debate that separate the 'clashes' which catch the headlines. An impression is created of irreconcilable hostility, and much parliamentary debate develops into a charade in which the audience believe more than the actors. We are so accustomed to it, that it has ceased to strike us as strange that our statesmen should be obliged to go about their business in a manner unparalleled in any other profession except that of the law. Elsewhere, in industry, commerce, medicine, the civil and armed services, science and education, the object is to minimize conflict; in politics the object is to augment it, and where it doesn't exist, to seek it out. No doubt one salutary effect of the charade on public men is to sharpen their powers of criticism, particularly of self-criticism, and to ensure that no errors of judgement or hint of dishonesty are allowed to pass unchallenged because of some unwritten rules of reticence or fair play. But the price they pay in terms of mental wear and tear, and the constant need to act out of character, is a heavy one. Most men have two personalities, private and public. A Minister must have five, in his house, in his office, in Parliament, in his constituency and when he faces his party loyalists in conference. The gulf between leaders and led is the same as the gulf between the second and fifth of these personalities.

The atmosphere of the party system is one of unceasing conflict between Us and Them, which increases in intensity the further down the political scale we go. Reputations and opinions are divided between whites and blacks, and the main object of party organizations is to paint out the intrusive grey over as large an area as possible. Everyone knows that the division between the two great parties on major issues simply reflects the division which exists in most men's minds. The party organization gets to work on the half of their minds which favours the course which the party leaders have decided to sponsor. Its task is not particularly difficult. The vast majority of party-members are only too anxious to agree, and many of them may become quite unaware that the temptation to disagree ever existed. Thus the battle to gain party support for a policy is already nine-tenths won by its mere enunciation. The appeal to loyalty, the desire to attack the traditional enemy wherever he may be found, the sense of belonging together, respect for leaders of proved efficiency and character—all of them military virtues—become substitutes for thought. The danger is that this largely automatic process of organizing party approval, which is an undoubted aid to steady government, may create the impression that thoughtfulness, reservations or open disagreement on the part of a few, are not inconvenient merely, but signs of disloyalty and even caddishness.

If politics are conceived in terms of a battle, the rules of battle must be held to apply. Loyalty to the leader must take precedence over any conflicting loyalty, and to oppose him at a difficult moment is as great an act of treachery as to shoot the Colonel in the back as he leads the troops into action. When faced by a real battle, such as a war or a major economic crisis, the electors are the first to demand a Coalition Government; and even on matters of importance to particular sections of the community, such as pensions or the future of Kenya, the cry is often raised, 'take it out of party politics'. It is an implied admission that party conflict is a luxury, an amusement, and, at least partially, a pretence, and that it should be restricted to areas where it can do little harm. But because such an admission is never specifically made, real and sham become inextricably confused. The dilemma has been well expressed by J. F. S. Ross:

The doctrine that there is a continuous natural division of political opinion into two streams and only two streams, left and right, is quite unsound. There is no such *natural* division: its existence is an illusion, originating in the accidents of history. . . . The true picture of the community's attitude to this or that political issue, is not that of a field of battle with two hostile armies facing each other across a deserted no-man's land. It is rather that of a crowd milling about in a park, with a fringe of rival speakers doing their best to attract the attention and secure the adherence of as many members of the crowd as they can.[1]

Not even the most combatant of politicians is entirely happy about the false picture he has constructed in his mind. A time must come in every man's life when he feels dissatisfied with what the party system is offering him, and his protest may take one of two forms. Either he says that his own party is being seduced by extremists of the right or left: that it is not he that has changed, but his party that has been transformed by heresy. Or he begins to doubt the validity of a system which crushes independent minds. Whichever his reaction, he is brought up against the problem of dissent. If he is a man of firm party allegiances, he is likely to by-pass the core of the problem by lamenting the extinction of the independent Member, who could express unorthodox points of view without harming the structure of either of the monolithic parties. He too rarely admits that the extinction of the independent Member is of less importance than the gradual erosion of independence itself within the two great parties, or that he has unconsciously contributed to it by his own strong partisanship in the past.

The vanished Independents have achieved in recollection a status which they seldom occupied in practice. Even their numbers have swollen in our imaginations. A study made by David Butler of independent membership of Parliament[2] revealed that excluding University Members, the total number of Independent Members returned at General Elections since the first war were: 1918, four; 1922, eleven; 1923, six; 1924, four; 1929, six; 1931, three; 1935, seven; 1945, fifteen; 1950, three; 1951, three. And in 1955, there were only the two Sinn Fein Members, neither of

[1] J. F. S. Ross, *Elections and Electors*. London, 1955, pp. 175–6.
[2] D. E. Butler, *The Electoral system in Britain 1918–1951*. Oxford, 1953, p. 154.

whom had any intention of taking their seats, even if they had been released from Belfast prison to do so. Even these figures, adds Mr Butler, 'give an exaggerated picture of those who success- fully defied the party machines. If only those candidates who defeated opponents from both the Conservative and Labour parties are considered, the following totals are left: 1918, nil; 1922, two; 1923, nil; 1924, nil; 1929, one; 1931, one; 1935, five; 1945, ten; 1950, nil; 1951, nil.' So apart from the wholly exceptional condi- tions of the 1945 election, when the long period of party truce had encouraged candidates to break away from the major parties, independent candidatures have been risky propositions for a long time, and it is no novelty that the electorate considers them largely irrelevant to the serious business of politics. Even the University seats, which in retrospect are assumed to have been filled by men independent of parties, usually returned Members who were com- mitted to support one or other of them. In the 1945 election the Universities elected six declared supporters of the previous Government, two near-Conservatives and only four genuine Independents. At the dissolution in 1950 the Conservatives had the sympathy, if not the allegiance, of nine out of the twelve University Members.

The reason for the decline, and eventual extinction, of the independent Members, is not so much that the great party machines deliberately set out to grind them to dust, as that possible supporters were discouraged by the assumption that they would fail, and by the fear that, if elected, they would be ineffec- tive in Parliament and therefore powerless to look after their con- stituents' interests. The expense of a modern election campaign is a sufficient deterrent to many lonely prospective candidates; to others it is the fear of ridicule. Independents have themselves often been the chief enemies of independence. Their pathetic optimism, the extraordinary policies for which they have can- vassed support, their eccentric methods of campaigning, have caused all Independents to be regarded with a certain pity or disdain. Mr H. C. Wright, for example, a Christian Evangelist who stood as an Independent at the North Dorset by-election in June 1957, did not make it any easier for his successors elsewhere by proclaiming at the outset of his campaign, 'Call me the atom-

man who gets things done: I shall get in with 22,000 votes.' He
received 170.

Even the most gallant independent candidatures, like that of
Sir Richard Acland at Gravesend in 1955, did not fail because the
voters were somehow intimidated by the official parties. Intimidation is impossible so long as the secrecy of the ballot is absolute.
Acland may have failed because his constituents disagreed with
him about the hydrogen bomb. It is more probable, however,
that his ill-success was due to an even profounder reason, namely,
that the British people wish to maintain the classic system, and
prefer a Member whose vote is tied at least at one end to predictable policies and identifiable leaders. There is a proper distrust of a multiplicity of parties each anxious to find new points of
difference from every other, and every independent Member is
potentially the nucleus of such a party. Besides, to vote for an
Independent, particularly at a General Election (in which Acland's
demonstration was unexpectedly confused), is to contract out of
the fascinating struggle between the two major parties. The elector
is denying himself the right to influence the choice of the next
Government. His vote is to that extent 'wasted'.

If the regret at the passing of the independent Members were
genuine, we might have expected to find that the electors were
anxious that their Members should compensate for it by acting with
reasonable freedom within the framework of the parties. In fact,
for a strong party-man to deplore the extinction of the Independents seems to be little more than an easy way of paying lip-service
to independence itself, in which he decreasingly believes. Those
who still cling to the idea of Parliament as an assembly where
judgement and integrity should count for more than mere
obedience, have often become disgusted with party, resigned
from their local party Associations or refused to join them, and
so left the field clear for the loyalists to enforce a discipline not
only over their local supporters, but sometimes over the Member
himself.

This idea is something quite new in British politics. It is a
spontaneous development within the great Party organizations
outside Parliament, not one fostered by the party leaders themselves. Members of the Government, members of opposition

shadow-Governments, and often the chairmen of national party organizations, have themselves been Members of Parliament for many years. They know the stresses to which Members are constantly subject. Almost all of them, at some point in their careers, have found it impossible to agree with the majority. They know that problems, which may seem so simple to the readers of headlines, are infinitely complicated, and that a monolithic response to the official line is quite unnatural to men whose whole careers are shaped by the weighing of evidence and forming of judgements. The more important the issue, the stronger will be the dissentient feelings aroused by it. But the very intensity with which party leaders are obliged to respond to challenge, the aggressive tone in which they frame their arguments, have concealed their respect for disagreement and led their imitators lower down the political scale to assume that victory is more important than truth.

It is a trend difficult to reverse. Sustained political attack cannot suddenly be unwound by its chief initiators. If they were to say in a periodic aside, 'By the way, you must discount a large part of what we are telling you; we have considerable doubts about it ourselves', there would only be confusion and dismay. It is left to common sense to make these reservations: they can never be explicitly stated. If common sense fails, and the charade is mistaken for the reality, the deviation can be corrected only by the subtlest and slowest political methods. Party supporters can no more be told that they have misunderstood their leaders' real intentions, than the leaders can admit that they have made a serious error of judgement.

Hitherto, there has been little discussion in political writings about the responsibilities of the electors, as opposed to their rights. Throughout the nineteenth century and in the early part of the twentieth, the gradual extension of the franchise, until it became universal, was a matter for mounting self-congratulation. Its partial withdrawal is now unthinkable, and any suggestion that it might be abused is a slap in the face of those who won it. The people cannot be wooed by insults. Nevertheless, two reminders should occasionally be given. The first is that the popular vote was never intended to operate continuously, by keeping Members of Parliament on a tight leash between elections. The second is that the party system was evolved in order to organize opinion, not to stamp it out from a mould.

If these two basic assumptions were ignored, there would be four main effects, none the less pernicious for becoming only very gradually apparent. A party would find it increasingly difficult to originate new ideas, or to adapt its old ones. Even its emotions would become stereotype. Its chief men would be survivors, not leaders. It would be held to be as great a virtue to obliterate minorities within the party as outside it; and since minorities seldom submit tamely to obliteration, a form of civil war would result, black looks and worse being exchanged between friends and colleagues, and the already artificially stimulated conflict of the parties would be reproduced, in far more bitter form, inside the party itself. Agreement would not result, only a particularly futile victory of the majority, which would be committed not to deviate from the arguments by which their victory had been won. Decent men would ultimately express their disgust by withdrawing from politics, which would have become an arena for professional matadors alone.

Secondly, a commercial relationship would arise between the Member and his constituents. You want the best seats, they would say; you can purchase them in the coin of obedience, for the survival and victory of the party is paramount over all niceties of individual conscience. I have used the word 'constituents'. If it were so, and if 65,000 people had an identifiable collective will, this doctrine, mistaken though I believe it to be, might be defended. But today, when a Member speaks of his constituents, he usually means those who voted for him; and since even they are not all identifiable, he means those who have openly joined his local party organization; or, as a further refinement, those who control it, a handful, it may ultimately be, of men and women, of passionate party loyalty, but no wide political experience, who have his fate in their hands. What man, it may be asked, would be prepared to surrender his opinion to theirs, not even with the excuse that they certainly represent the inarticulate majority? Yet already it is constantly done. By surrendering, he is not only belittling himself and Parliament. He is betraying those thousands of people inside his own party who share the qualms which he dare not express. For though in name he may be the Member for Bristol alone, he is also the spokesman for others scattered throughout the country who may not even know of his existence, but are hoping to hear some voice raised in Parliament on their behalf. It would be an absurdity if party dissent could not be expressed at Westminster in at least the same proportions as it is expressed in the country, merely because each individual Member thought himself bound, at all costs, to take his directions from the inner ring in his constituency to whom he originally owed his seat. The commercial deal would not only be squalid and humiliating; it would frustrate the claim of Parliament to be a mirror of the nation.

A third effect of binding the Member too tightly to party, locally or nationally, by extracting promises or by making threats, is to make it almost impossible for him to act as a curb upon the executive, if his own party happens to be in power. This, after all, is one of his main functions. If he accepts the argument of his more militant supporters, that the Cabinet, being composed of men of exceptional ability and proved party loyalty, must be trusted absolutely on all great issues, then he is unconsciously accepting the fundamental thesis of dictatorship. One of the assumptions of democracy is that Ministers can make mistakes. When confronted by a conflict of election pledges, for example, in circumstances which could not have been foreseen at the election, they may choose to honour the wrong one. In the urgency of the crisis, they need both the support and the advice of Members on their back benches, who are close enough to the crisis to understand its ramifications, but far enough away, and with sufficient leisure for reflection, to judge whether something more valuable is being thrown away by the proposed action than gained. If the need for action is so immediate, or secrecy is so important that they cannot consult their back-benchers beforehand, the latter should not consider themselves gagged by the *fait accompli*. Their desire to save the Government embarrassment is simply an extra restraint upon their criticisms, not an ultimate barrier upon any criticism whatever.

Fourthly, it may happen that a Member attaches great importance to a particular principle or facet of his party's policy, and legitimately emphasized it in his own election address and speeches. In a marginal seat he might even have owed his victory to the individual gloss he put upon it, appealing to one section of the uncommitted vote; or it might have been a central reason why he first joined his party, and stood for Parliament in its name. Such a consideration might be his party's traditional conduct of foreign affairs, or its attitude to the poor. If a decision of his party seems an affront to everything he has ever preached on the subject, nothing should prevent him from saying so. At that moment, particularly, he represents all his constituents, not merely his supporters. He would be doing a great disservice to Parliament and to his constituency if he kept silent. It is in the knowledge that Members with that degree of conviction sit on the back-benches that party leaders frame and modify their policies. They do not resent, though they may often regret, its expression.

In short, a severe limitation on a Member's right to say what he thinks on the issues which stir him most deeply, would diminish both the authority of Parliament and the vigour of parties. It would lead to sullen acquiescence in public and bitter feuds in private. Confronted by the choice between political frustration and political suicide, many Members would choose frustration. All of them have their careers, and some their livelihoods, to consider. But it is wrong that they should ever be asked to make such a choice. It is not necessary. Members have rarely abused the right to a reasonable degree of freedom. They wish their party to succeed. They have so often argued its case, that they have come to believe even in its exaggerations. They respect their leaders, in whose appointment, directly or indirectly, they have probably played some part, and for their constituents it is rare that they cannot feel, even in moments of tribulation, both affection and regard. They realize that self-restraint is essential, for there is a limit beyond which heresy cannot be tolerated if the party is to survive, and those who find themselves consistently or temperamentally at logger-heads with their colleagues, would be better outside it. Thus, there is every natural incentive to conform; every natural obstacle to dissent. Only when most strongly impelled would they make use of their freedom, and they should not be denied it by their local party supporters when they are not denied it by their leaders.

Political intolerance is not everywhere. In the larger number of constituencies there is mutual trust and good-will between the Member and his local party organization. It is only in some constituencies, usually those with big majorities, that tolerance has suffered a check, and the habit may spread. At the moment, except in a few places, it is underground. It takes the form of a whispering campaign against the Member, that he is too left for a Conservative or too right for a Socialist; for one of the more alarming aspects of the new trend is that there is seldom any danger to a Member who is on the extremist wing of either party. Unknown even to their party headquarters or to more than a handful of their colleagues, Members are fighting week-end by week-end despairing battles against such whispering campaigns. Here is one, a Conservative, whose wholly innocent visit to Russia has caused heads to nod in confirmation of what was always suspected, that 'he is not entirely trustworthy'. Here a Labour Member, whose speech on unofficial strikes, though consistent with party doctrine, has set his more militant supporters looking around for another candidate. These are actual examples. How can either man give of his best, if constantly worried by such disapproval?

Members of Parliament have always complained in private, though they may sometimes have boasted in public, that they are the servants of their constituents. As far back as 1742 the electors of Bath could issue this thinly veiled threat to their two Members: 'These are our sentiments, ye are our representatives, and we are yr. electors.'[1] By 1911, when Belloc wrote his philippic against the party system, the caucus had replaced the whole body of electors as the main menace to Members' integrity: 'They must be prepared to defend not only an existing programme, settled between the various officials and professional politicians, but any future decisions which their superiors may feel inclined to take.'[2] Belloc's caucus was central, not local. His worst fears were not realized, but transformed. It is no longer the professional party managers, but their followers, loyally acting as they suppose that

[1] Quoted by C. S. Emden, *The People and the Constitution*. Oxford, 1933.
[2] Hilaire Belloc and Cecil Chesterton, *The Party System*. London, 1911.

the managers would wish them to act, who are distorting the true purpose of the party system. Because the managers, and even the victims themselves, say nothing to correct the prevailing view that Members are elected primarily to support the party on every occasion, it gathers strength, and confusion spreads.

Even if we had a written constitution, a relationship so subtle as that between a Member and his constituents could never be defined in Britain as sharply as it was in Article 21 of the constitution of the Weimar Republic: 'Deputies are representatives of the whole people. They are subject to their conscience only, and are not bound by any instructions.' This is a declaration which, in our eyes, shirks far too many of the problems of a democracy. But in the absence of any precise definition of principle, we must be all the more careful about our practice. We must watch the shifts of power, and note their effects. Instead of mumbling aphorisms from Burke, whose great speeches and writings on the subject are more often quoted than understood, we must sort out by analysis of actual instances, and categories of political events, where the Member's duty lies, and where the rights of his electors. We want a temporary answer only, but one which will reduce to proper proportions the competing claims of people and Parliament, when both of them think they know best.

Chapter Two

THE MEMBER
AND HIS CONSTITUENTS

Local party organization—reasons for joining a political party—consistency and conformity—those who vote for a party but do not join it—the local party leaders and workers—loyalty—the advantages of a local party organization—autonomy of constituency parties—the dangers of docility—selection of candidates—nursing a seat—mutual sympathy between Members and their constituents—importance of curiosity and accessibility—non-political links with constituency—how to become popular and unpopular—a General Election—present methods of appealing to voters are too crude—the party conference—Conservative and Labour conferences compared—different attitudes to party-system of Members and party-workers—quarrels between Members and their constituencies—when should a Member be dismissed?—should he then stand as an Independent?—Mr Churchill and the Epping Division

ALL CONSTITUENTS ARE electors; most are consistent supporters of one party; comparatively few join their local party organization by paying an annual subscription; still fewer play any active part in its affairs; and of those who do, a small knot of energetic men and women run the machine and control its policy. A Conservative Association in a constituency of 65,000 may have 11,000 paid-up members or only a few hundred: the average is about 5,000. It is governed by an Executive Council of about forty members. A Labour constituency party is considerably smaller, because many potential members are already affiliated to the Labour Party through their Trades Unions. But the effect is the same. The local organization is kept alive by the energy of a few people who speak in the name of the whole body of supporters. They are fully entitled to such local prestige as their offices carry, since the rewards for their service are otherwise meagre. Financially their devotion is a liability.

The stages by which a man turns from luke-warm supporter into front-line campaigner are stages in the intensification, rather than in the deepening, of his political faith. Few of us could say that we joined our party after profound self-examination. We usually joined because our friends joined, or because there was a long family tradition, or because social circumstances steered us naturally in that direction. Having joined, we are reluctant to change, and we spend the rest of our lives explaining to ourselves and each other why we could never have done anything else. The arguments, in fact, usually come long after the decision. Political parties consciously or unconsciously work on this foible. To change a vote between one election and the next is an admission that we were wrong last time, either because we failed to see through the promises of the party for which we voted, or because we have since discovered that its policies, when carried out in full, have had less agreeable results than we had imagined. As few people wish to make such an admission, the party vote is already heavily weighted by electors who think it not only disloyal, but irresolute, to change their minds. The argument that it may be quite consistent for an elector to change his party, because his party has meanwhile changed its character, is one which candidates might more frequently employ to break into the solid voting strength of their opponents.

Consistency is the strongest motive for the vote. Second to it comes the desire to conform to the opinions of the people with whom we come daily into contact.

'The knowledge of agreement with fellow members of his group,' wrote Mark Benney, 'whether family, circle of friends, or colleagues at work, further strengthens a person's already strong inclination to stand by his established convictions. . . . Conversions through open argument, while they undoubtedly occur sometimes, are comparatively infrequent, and social groups move towards unanimity through much more indirect means—for example, through the suggestive power of the implicit assumption of agreement which forms a background to much political discussion, and is accompanied by hostile references to the supporters of opposing parties, giving a veiled threat of ostracism if the listener should be one of them.'[1]

How well a politician recognizes that 'implicit assumption of agreement'! Often a chance meeting with some acquaintance who puts on that special tone of voice will be enough to decide a person's attitude to a complicated issue which has just burst into the headlines. When it is maintained for year after year in an

[1] Mark Benney, A. P. Gray and R. H. Pear, *How People Vote*. London, 1956, p. 185.

entire neighbourhood, only a person of unusual strength of character, or a malicious desire to be different, will resist it.

A party's voting strength is based on these two scruples, consistency and conformity. If a voter can be persuaded actually to join the party by paying a subscription, both are reinforced, for he has now publicly declared his allegiance. Perhaps the subscription was only handed over at the door-step to get rid of an importunate canvasser. No matter. He is now on a list. He has voluntarily surrendered the secrecy of his ballot paper. It will be doubly difficult for him to break faith.

What of those who never join? Numerically they average four out of every five Conservatives, and nine out of ten Socialists, if we discount Trades Union affiliation. They may never have been canvassed for a subscription, or they were not able to afford it; or they contributed directly to national party funds; or they had not yet made up their minds how to vote; or they wished to keep their political opinions to themselves; or they disliked the local Member or agent, or one of his branch officers; or they had just moved into the district, or were about to leave; or they did not wish to be involved, however remotely, in the intrigues inseparable from local party politics. There are a dozen possible reasons. But it does not mean that their opinions can be ignored when an issue flares up within a constituency affecting every person who supports the party, whether by subscription or by vote. It might be argued that if they wished to have any influence on what is done, they should take the trouble to join. That argument would apply to a musical society or a tennis club; but it cannot apply to a political organization, when many of the reasons for not joining it are quite consistent with support for the party's interests. A chairman is obliged to listen for these outside voices and to be influenced by them, not only because they are in a majority and he is speaking in their name, but because the attitude of those who do not join is likely to be more moderate than the attitude of those who do.

Most active members of an Association are women, and many of them have reached their middle-age. They have the time to spare, and feel the want of exactly the type of social intercourse for a high purpose which their membership brings. They are capable of deep loyalty, and intense dislikes. They prefer their politics clean-cut. When they attend a meeting to hear the Member or another party spokesman, they are apt to be disconcerted by a novel approach which throws doubt on what they have previously heard and repeated. They do not share the outsider's objections to political truisms emphatically delivered, and condemnation of the party's prominent opponents has become as much a ritual of such meetings as praise for its leaders. It is a heady atmosphere, easy to recreate, difficult to dispel. But for most of the time, politics is not the immediate concern of these little groups which keep the party system alive. The political address occupies the same place in their activities as the sermon in the lives of good Christians. It is a stiffener of established faith. Perhaps one meeting out of four is for the purpose of talking politics. The others are either purely social occasions, with tea, a whist drive or lantern lecture, or to discuss future activities such as the stall which the branch has agreed to run for the Christmas bazaar. Though non-political, these small functions create political cohesion in a local party by bringing the same people together at regular intervals in circumstances which they enjoy.

Their leaders are not always the natural leaders of the district, who may be too busy with their own affairs, or indifferent to the small beer of local politics. They are to be found among men and women who seek nothing more than a useful outlet for their energies, and an association with the great figures and events of the day. If asked why they give up so much time to an activity in which the rewards are so small and the frustrations so many, they would probably answer that they 'believe in the party'. This is undoubtedly true. But the amount of effort they give to thinking about the party's purposes is inevitably far less than the attention they pay to the running of their part of the machine. Outsiders, insiders, and the party's headquarters, will judge them not by the originality or profundity of their ideas, but by the number of paid-up members which they can declare annually, and by the efficiency of their organization when the election comes. Particularly is this so of the agent, the only salaried member of a team of amateurs, who is not expected, nor even allowed, to have views of his own on party policy, and spends his whole time organizing support for the policies which are handed down to him from above. As he is the main initiator of action, the whole Association is coloured by his outlook. If there is a row between or within branches which drags on month after month, he is failing in his job. There will be enough of these clashes of personality to keep him busy without adding to them by stimulating clashes on policy. So a smooth-running machine, which is the desire of every chairman and agent, is one in which dissent of all sorts is discouraged, and social activities predominate over political. When in trouble, their instinct is to fall back on loyalty to the party's immediate interests. Just as it is the Cabinet's duty to preserve a united front in public, so it is the duty of the smallest unit in the party's organization at moments of crisis to keep together on the basis of agreement with what they are advised.

In my own constituency, there is a highly valued member who has beaten all regional records for enrolling new members. Over a period of years he has brought thousands into the Association by knocking importunately at their doors. A modest, though indefatigable, man, he cannot believe that the leaders for whom he has worked so hard could ever be guilty of a serious error of judgement. So, faithful to a fault, *plus royaliste que le Roi*, he regards deviations within his own party as an enormity ten times more dreadful than forthright opposition to it from outside. I doubt whether he will ever forgive me for my own two major criticisms of official Conservative policy. I owe more to this man than to any other individual locally. He has done more than I have ever done myself to strengthen the Conservative hold on my seat. When things went right, I gladly accepted his support, and never questioned whether it was based on deep conviction or simple acquiescence. He never asked for gratitude, only that I should always fight on the same side as himself; and while he has never failed me, he considers that I have failed him: I was telling each of his thousand recruits that they had made a big mistake. It is useless for me to reply that two criticisms do not amount to total rejection. In his eyes they do.

It would be wrong to class together such devoted party-workers with the militant extremists who represent but a tiny proportion of party membership. Paradoxically, keen party-members do not

2

usually hold strong political views of their own. They want the party to win locally and nationally, and they maintain that the arguments by which it wins are matters for the party leaders. It is tempting to say that the leaders are the strategists, and the constituency workers are the tacticians, of the campaign; but even this analogy would be false. The workers are more like the administrative services in an army than its assault troops. They do not normally raid the enemy's trenches. Open disagreement at a hostile doorstep or at a rival's meetings is the least of their weapons. They organize success by identifying their friends beforehand, committing them to vote by taking their subscriptions, making it easy for them to maintain their allegiance, and proclaiming to the world at large that this is a vigorous party with a large membership and strong leadership, which is likely to win. In the assumption of victory lies their greatest strength, for people wish to take part in a triumph, even when it is expected.

I have often asked myself whether the effort expended on the annual round of committees, fêtes, socials, brains-trusts and occasional public meetings, produces anything more than the agent's salary and office expenses, with a small surplus left over for central party funds. How many people would vote differently at an election if the whole apparatus were to be swept away? By misfortune, I am in a better position than most to answer that question, for I have had the full backing of an Association which was later marshalled against me.

In the first place, an Association provides a platform from which the Member can speak to the electorate at large. A speech heard by a bare dozen will be brought to the attention of thousands in the local newspaper, and though it may be read by very few, the headline is a reminder of the Member's existence, activity, and the support on which he can call. There are, of course, other platforms, but all too often the invitations to mount them are accompanied by the warning, 'Of course, I need not remind you that our rules forbid any mention of politics.' On one occasion, I was asked to speak about the international situation, 'but please *no politics.*' The branches may become bored by the details of current political controversies, but they can scarcely treat them as something improper. It was extremely useful to have these

recurrent opportunities to speak on topical events, and I greatly
miss them today.

Secondly, I miss the assistance of the agent and his staff. He
knows the constituency far better than I do. Among his many
other duties, he interposed a buffer between myself and the
cranks and people with insoluble grievances who are apt to flood
into a local constituency office. I now have to deal with them
alone. The agent is also an extremely useful one-man intelligence
service. Not only can he warn his Member of political issues
which are causing trouble locally, or are likely to cause it, but he
is the first to know of any personal quarrels among members of
the Association which the Member must be careful not to in-
tensify by a chance remark, and he can suggest a letter of con-
dolence, a greetings telegram, a note of apology or of congratula-
tion, which help to keep relations within a constituency healthy.
The office itself—a shop window for the party, a convenient
meeting place for committees, a centre for inquiries and an inter-
viewing room where constituents can see their Member at week-
ends—is a symbol of permanence and authority. When its doors
were closed to me, I realized its advantages far more acutely than
when I had freely enjoyed them.

But the greatest drawback of exclusion is undoubtedly the
magnetic tug which a local party organization exerts on all who
belong to it. As in most other forms of association, whether social
or functional, a constituency party is run by a few energetic people
who are re-elected annually to their offices as long as their
enthusiasm and patience induce them to stand. The rest are happy
to follow them, partly from reluctance to pit their wits against
more formidable personalities, partly from lack of time to replace
them or energy to engage in controversy, but mainly because the
party exists in order to agree; so a decision taken by very few is
endorsed by very many, and once it is taken, it becomes the
decision of thousands who would probably have been prepared
to acclaim an opposite decision had it been presented to them at
the start. The more sharply the decision is attacked from outside,
the greater the cohesion becomes inside. This instinctive locking
of shields in face of danger is of enormous value to a political
party, and nobody who has profited from it, as I have profited on

many occasions in the past, would think of mocking at it when he finds himself unhappily outside the ring. This spirit cannot be created overnight. It cannot be evoked like a genie for the purposes of elections only, and be stored in a jar for the three or four years between them. However mundane the activities of a normal con- stituency party may seem, they are part of a continuous process of creating mutual confidence, evolving leaders, and impressing out- siders by an assumption of success.

In both major parties, the local organization is autonomous. It raises and manages its own funds, selects its own candidates for local and national elections, plans and executes the election cam- paign, chooses its delegates to attend the party conference, and to a very large extent can put its own interpretation on party doctrine and ethics without forfeiting its membership of the national party. The Labour Party is rather stricter than the Con- servative. Labour constituency parties, for example, are obliged to adopt the party's model rules: Conservative Associations are only recommended to do so. In the Labour Party, an individual may be expelled by the local General Management Committee, but he has a right of appeal to the National Executive Committee: in the Conservative Party he has no such right. On the other hand, a dispute within a Conservative Association can be referred to a general meeting of all its members, while a constituency Labour party rarely meets as a single body, the ward members having delegated their powers to their representatives on the GMC, a procedure which must handicap any person anxious to appeal over the heads of the GMC to the wider, and possibly more moderate, opinion of local party-members outside the controlling ring. Occasions have occurred when an entire constituency Labour party has been disaffiliated by the NEC, following a refusal to disavow its Member who has fallen into disgrace with the party's leadership. But though the National Union has on paper the same right to withdraw its approval from a Conservative Association, I know of no instance when this has been done.[1] The disciplinary powers of the Conservative Central Office are even less than those of the National Union. The Maxwell-Fyfe report on party organi- zation, published in 1949, stated explicitly that 'no orders can be

[1] See R. T. McKenzie, *British Political Parties*. London, 1955, p. 242.

given to constituency Associations either by the Central Office or by the Area offices.'

As McKenzie points out in his careful analysis of the distribution of power within the two main Parties, 'in both cases effective power and authority is concentrated in the hands of the leaders of the party in Parliament.' How can this be reconciled with the autonomy of the local organizations? It is as if the battalions of an army were under no compulsion to carry out the orders of the army commander. The system can only be made to work on a basis of trust. The constituencies are trusted not to interfere with policy-making, and to concentrate their activities on winning votes. The leaders are trusted not to frame policies which put too great a strain on the loyalty of their supporters. Constituents have almost universally accepted the modest role allotted to them. There is little demand in either party to dictate policy from below, and less among the Conservatives than among their opponents. The semblance of a share in policy-making is given by the educational activities of the Conservative Party, but it is left deliberately vague who is educating whom. If the general body of party members are educating their leaders, they certainly have no power to compel attention to the lessons. 'The functions of the National Union,' says the Maxwell-Fyfe report, 'are primarily deliberative and advisory. . . . Its views are *conveyed* to the Leader or Chairman of the party.' (My italics.) In fact, as one would expect, the flow of ideas is mainly from above to below, from the professional to the volunteer.

Far from causing strain within the party, the system works so smoothly, and the division of functions appears so natural, that there is more danger in the docility of the constituency Associations than in their latent power, for they are tempted, as a matter of duty, to crush any deviationism within their ranks. They form an image, sometimes a false image, of what they think the party leaders stand for, and then, by procrustean methods, adapt their views to conform to that image. This is a development of the party system which even Belloc can never have foreseen. It would have been less surprising, with the immense growth in popular education, if the constituencies had rebelled against the assumption that they had no right or power to enforce their own views when

they differed from those of the party leaders. In the Conservative
Party, it might have seemed to them anachronistic that the Leader
was under no obligation to do more than listen. In the Labour
Party, it might have been deeply resented that the total constituency vote was still less than that of the single greatest Trades
Union. It might also have been expected that the constituency
parties would have demanded some voice in the election of their
national leaders. That they have made none of these demands
shows remarkable self-restraint. In compensation, they ask to be
left alone to manage their own affairs, and a bargain has been
implicitly struck upon that basis.

The most important of all the rights of a local political party is
the right to select their own candidate for a parliamentary election.
Implicit in it is the right to change him for another if he fails to
satisfy them, whether he was successful in the election or not. But
an original choice is usually the final choice, until the Member or
candidate decides that he wishes to give up politics, or (very rarely
in the case of a Member) that he would prefer to contest another
seat.

The selection of a candidate is not only the local party's most
important right; it is also their most important duty. Upon the
type of man the constituencies choose will depend the quality of
Parliament, and they are choosing not for a single Parliament, but,
by implication, for a whole series of Parliaments. A man who has
had the good fortune to be selected for a seat with a big majority
is usually regarded as safe for life. This applies to about two-
thirds of all the seats in the country, disregarding such hazards as
boundary changes, or the building of a vast new housing estate,
which can present the seat accidentally to the other side. To
secure the dominant party's nomination for such a seat is virtually
the equivalent of election to Parliament: the election itself is a
formality. It is seldom recognized that the majority of Members
are thus chosen not by the votes of the people, but by the necessarily haphazard methods of a party selection committee, who
present their candidate to the general body of their supporters as
the ensign of the colour: *nunc plaudite omnes.*

They are not entirely free in their choice. Both party head-quarters reserve the ultimate right to veto, as they reserve the right to suggest, a candidate. The Labour Party rules declare that 'the selection of a prospective parliamentary candidate shall not be regarded as completed until his name has been placed before a meeting of the National Executive Committee, and his selection has been duly endorsed.' It has happened, for instance in the case of the Thurrock division in 1949, that the NEC have instructed the constituency Labour party to select a new prospective candidate in place of the sitting Member who had displeased the party leaders.[1] But such strong measures are extremely rare. It is normally enough for the elections sub-committee of the NEC to discourage the adoption of a particular candidate, for their advice to be taken. On the other hand, pressure from head office to take a man whom the Parliamentary Labour Party would like to have at Westminster is likely to harm his chances, as the case of Tom Driberg, Chairman of the Party, but rejected by the St Helen's Labour party in April 1958, amply proved.

In the Conservative Party approval normally precedes adoption. The Central Office maintains a list of suitable candidates which is sent on request to Associations. The Maxwell-Fyfe report acknowledged their right to select a candidate not on the list, but 'in that case, the Association should see that the candidate receives the approval of the Standing Advisory Committee on Parliamentary Candidates before adoption as prospective candidate takes place;' in other words, during the interval between his selection by the local Executive and the confirmation of his candidature by a general meeting of the Association. It is naturally not revealed how often Central Office approval has been withheld. It must be a very rare event, for in cases of doubt, the Party Chairman will have had wind of an Association's intentions through his area agent, and privately warned them off a wholly unsuitable choice. As in the Labour Party, such advice would be heeded, though a strong hint from Central Office, or from an individual party leader, that a particular candidate would be welcomed in high places, is likely to cause more resentment than gratitude. In effect, then, the preferences of the constituency party organiza-

[1] See McKenzie, p. 528.

tions, exercisable within these very wide limits, will determine the character of the party in Parliament.

For a seat with a good majority which the sitting Member has decided to hand over to a successor, the competition is very keen, particularly at a by-election following soon after a General Election at which many career-parliamentarians have lost their seats. About a hundred names might be submitted for such a candidature, half of which will have been suggested by head-quarters. Others will write in hopefully on their own account, and some will use local connections to advance their claims. In the Conservative Party the mass of papers is sorted out by a small selection committee of five or six, including the chairman of the local party and possibly the retiring Member himself. From the hundred, they will pick out a short list of half a dozen whom they will invite to attend a full meeting of the Executive Council, a body composed of all the Association's officers and branch officers, some forty or fifty people in all. Each prospective-prospective candidate will address them in turn.

I have appeared before three such Executives—in Leicester, in the Camborne division of Cornwall, and in Bournemouth—and the procedure and atmosphere of each was very similar. It is a gala occasion for the selectors; slow torture for the candidates. So great is the strain of maintaining an amicable conversation with his rivals and their wives, that it is a relief for the applicant to leave the ante-room and follow the agent into the main hall for the ten-or twenty-minute interview which may alter the entire direction of his life. The audience already knows a great deal about him, but he cannot be sure quite what they know. Normally, a candidate makes the most of all favourable facts which are not likely to be contradicted by the more impartial summary of his life-story which the selectors hold in their hands. They do not want a speech about party policy. They want to discover what sort of person he is, or is capable of pretending to be, for most people can conceal the less agreeable sides of their natures for so short a period. If they cannot, they will not make good politicians, and deserve to lose.

I am doubtful whether I was the most suitable candidate on any of my three short-lists. In Leicester, I was alarmingly in-experienced. In Cornwall, one of my rivals knew the district intimately and was in other ways excellently equipped to represent it in the House of Commons. In Bournemouth, one of the most eminent economists in the country had offered himself for the seat, and by this time he would certainly have become a Minister of importance. The Cornishman was rejected because he was momentarily overcome by nerves in the course of his speech; the economist, I suspect, because he bored the Council with a lecture on finance, and could not promise to live in the constituency. In other words, the choice was determined by considerations which were transitory.

The complaint is often made that selection committees tend to choose people like themselves, and to demand of them promises which are inconsistent with the purpose of Parliament. It has even been said that in both the Conservative and Labour parties a candidate must promise complete and absolute party obedience, before he can be selected. Having questioned many Members about their experiences, I have only found one, a Conservative, who was asked for this undertaking, and he deeply regrets having given it. Nor is it true that members of selection committees suspect abilities which they do not happen to possess themselves. Naturally they look out for qualities and attitudes which reflect their own aspirations, but no member of a committee would be satisfied with a candidate who was not capable of rising to greater heights of oratory or influence than himself, and nothing pleases a constituency more than the appointment of their own Member to positions of distinction. At the same time he must be human and likeable. An intellectual or a business-man without any apparent interest in the problems or recreations of ordinary people, and who seems likely to treat his constituency merely as a stepping-stone to high office, will stand little chance in either party. At one time the Conservatives were apt to demand a big financial contribution to an Association as the price of a seat, but since their post-war reform which limits a Member's contribution to £50 a year, this abuse seems only to exist in some sections of the Labour Party.[1] In short, constituency parties seek able men

---

[1] 'There is danger in the growing practice of local Labour parties that their candidates should pay handsomely towards the cost of the election. How wrong this

to represent them, and it would be wrong to suggest that they perform their most important function selfishly.

The drawback of the system is that so small a body of people should have an effective voice in choosing so large a proportion of the present membership of Parliament. That there is no articulate protest against this practice is a measure of the private Member's declining importance and of the party's mounting authority. It does not matter to nine-tenths of the electorate what sort of men the candidates are, so long as each can display his official party ticket. The vote is given to the party, not to the man. One of the most successful politicians I know has told me that he cannot claim to have won personally more than five hundred votes in a constituency which he has represented for more than twelve years. If a method could be found to spread more widely the responsibility for choosing the candidate, there would be more public discussion of the qualities needed in a Member of Parliament, greater understanding that there can be a legitimate difference of attitude and opinion between two men speaking in the name of the same party, and a more intelligent approach to the election itself.

Those who believe in proportional representation think that their system would have this result. The alternative vote might do so, but proportional representation might have the very opposite result, by making the candidate an even more nebulous figure than he is already. A group of candidates would be standing for a group of seats. They would not have time to make themselves known individually to many hundreds of thousands, and when the election was over, the valuable relationship between a Member and a fixed body of constituents, who are his responsibility alone, would be lost. Several Members would represent everybody in a large district. The polling-figures for the two-member seats, which were only finally abolished in 1946, prove that only a fraction of one per cent of the electors would cast their second votes for a different party than their first, however much the quality of the candidates might vary. If the number of candi-

is—above all for Labour. It erects a financial barrier between bright young men and service in Parliament.' Wilfred Fienburgh, MP, *Sunday Pictorial*, September 18th, 1955.

dates were to be multiplied, and the electoral unit were extended from a single constituency to many, a confused electorate would be forced back on their only sure guide, the party label.

There is no need for any revolutionary reform. It is only necessary for the party headquarters to encourage selection of the candidate on a wider basis and over a longer period. After the local Executive Council have reduced applicants to a short-list, a general meeting of the Association or constituency party should make the choice. If the election is near, it would be necessary for this to be a final choice. But if it is several years ahead, the candidate should be regarded as on trial. It is true that he would have no security, but politics is not a profession which ranks security high among its attractions. Nobody should be able to win a seat in Parliament by an adroit performance at a twenty-minute interview which only one in a thousand electors can attend. He should be obliged to work for his seat, make his views known on the whole range of political issues, put his personal qualities to the test of widely different circumstances, and not feel disgruntled if he is not selected in the end. When time is available and competition is keen, two prospective candidates might run in harness for a year, addressing each of the branches in turn, and familiarizing themselves with the constituency. Each would naturally gain a body of supporters. But there is no reason to fear a split in the party organization, provided that it was understood from the start that a final decision was to be made between them in a year's time by a secret ballot confined to paid-up members of the local party, and that the loser, like the losers in the present selection process, would transfer all his support to the winner, and melt away from the local political scene.

Once the selection-committee have made their choice, and he has been acclaimed by a meeting of the whole local party, there is a moment of deep, shared satisfaction. The selectors have completed an arduous task, and congratulate themselves in congratulating him. The successful candidate, ignoring the ugly prefix 'prospective' which belittles his status, sees himself more than half-way to membership of the House of Commons. His first

tour of the constituency with the agent fills him with delight.
'Those streets, those villages, are *mine*! They will vote for *me*!'
Aware that first impressions endure, he will assume his constituency smile as soon as he crosses its boundaries, and relax it
only in his hotel room or in the train which bears him away. It is
his moment of greatest enthusiasm. He wishes to know everything, everyone. Each ward meeting is a renewal of his triumph.
He watches the newspapers for any hint of an election which will
complete it. The sitting Member, if of the opposite party, suddenly becomes a clay figure in which he will stick innumerable
pins.

It is after the first enthusiasm has passed that the candidate will
need to collect all his reserves of energy and good temper. The
second time round the party branches is apt to reveal some of the
tedium and difficulties which he will encounter increasingly during
his period of incubation. Few people are sufficiently interested in
him even to inquire his name. His candidature is not, as he at first
imagined, a key to all doors. Even the Inland Revenue do not
recognize his heavy travelling, lodging and entertainment
expenses as a proper claim against Income Tax. He must expect
rebuffs outside the small circle where he is a hero, and a gradual
cooling off of admiration and solicitude within it. It is then that
he must take the lead, establish himself as the main originator of
ideas for improving the party's local organization and interesting
the public, put on its correct footing his relationship with his
chairman and agent, and strive, quite deliberately, to make himself
liked.

To be liked by his chief constituency supporters, whether as
candidate or Member, is more important than for him to be
admired. Their affection for him is the reserve on which he will
need to draw in moments of crisis. But they will not like him
unless he likes them. 'It is important to have a respect and not a
contempt for the general body of good citizens,' wrote Mr
Herbert Morrison. 'It is undesirable to cultivate a vindictive
relish in offending the susceptibilities (even if mistaken) of large
numbers of one's fellow citizens. . . . One cannot effectively serve
the people unless one likes them.'[1] Liking, in this sense, certainly

[1] Herbert Morrison, *Government and Parliament*. Oxford, 1954, p. 169.

does not mean a false display of fellowship. 'The very attempt towards pleasing everybody,' said Edmund Burke, 'discovers a temper always flashy and false and insincere.' The Member and candidate must not be frightened of showing that he can be moved to anger with a constituent. From time to time he should reveal the bed-rock within him, the mettle which Winston Churchill has extolled as one of the most estimable qualities in a man. Beyond that, he requires ordinary politeness, an average gift for concealing boredom, good humour, and a capacity for relating names to faces.

The key to his relationship with his constituents is found in Mr Morrison's word 'respect'. It means not only good manners, but interest and concern. A Member will start his career with a great advantage if he has in him a fund of curiosity about other people, and is able to demonstrate it without impertinence: curiosity about personal problems, curiosity to know how the fire-brigade works or how New Forest ponies survive the winter, to go down a tin-mine or to milk a cow, curiosity about people and things so unassumed and sympathetic that he can sincerely say, as once I heard a wise man say, 'Nobody, except one person in a thousand, is a bore, and he is interesting because he is one person in a thousand.'

Curiosity may sound a cold attribute to put so near the top of a list of a politician's qualifications. But the lack of it will make him colder, and his job intolerable. People, except those who know him well or who regard all politicians as butts for ribaldry or abuse, tend to be shy of their representative. His mind, they wrongly imagine, is too full of great affairs and unrepeatable secrets for him to have time for their small troubles and thin ideas. So the candidate, and *a fortiori* the Member, must always be prepared to make the first advance, on their territory and not on his own, and with the object of discovering what they think and what they can tell him. He must, above all, rid himself of any temptation to despise ignorance or an inability to debate, when his own knowledge and articulateness are so often matters of mere opportunity. When, after a long discussion in Parliament, the Member returns to his constituency to hear the same subject treated in oversimplified and often prejudiced terms, he is inclined

to despair of that 'general will' which is supposed to guide his
actions. It is not so much his electors' lack of basic information
which sometimes dismays him, as an unwillingness to listen to
contrary argument, and an obstinate clinging to a point of view
which, to his own satisfaction, he has utterly demolished. Impatience at this stage is both rude and foolish. It will do him much
harm. Just because he is known to be better equipped dialecti-
cally, he is expected to win his arguments, and many of those
with whom he disputes on his home-ground will instinctively
stiffen their attitudes at the start, and the greater his destructive
skill, the deeper it will drive them into concrete emplacements of
prejudice. No man is at his best when conscious of his inferiority
in argument. No man enjoys being robbed of a point-of-view
which is part of a perhaps limited mental stock-in-trade. He will
defend even a completely untenable thesis because he will feel the
poorer without it, and irritability is the worst instrument with
which to attempt to prise it from him.

The purpose of such discussions, possibly the most valuable
part of a Member's experience, and certainly of a candidate's, is
not to win arguments but to create bonds of sympathy. Constituents are quick to detect conceit or indifference. He must be
equally quick to recognize genuine doubt and to distinguish
between disagreement and hostility. If a group of his constituents
remain deaf to his suggestions, let him reflect on the approval he
accords to others who accept his views without question, and
ask himself whether he is to be trusted absolutely with their trust.
Has he, too, not often been guilty of stubbornness with a Minister,
of over-simplification, of lack of generosity in argument? He
should know that far-fetched criticism is often no more than a
plain man's short-cut to originality, or a shy man's method of
escape from shyness. Criticism of this kind is preferable to a lazy
acceptance of a party platitude, devised in some back-room of the
party headquarters or popular newspaper, and reissued shop-
soiled across the bar of the local political club.

A candidate has this disadvantage compared to the Member,
that he is invariably identified with his party. The Member is 'our
MP'. Before he reaches Parliament he is 'the Tory candidate'. This
slightly pejorative label cuts him off from half his constituents.

Having no power and little influence to help them, the candidate is in the unenviable position of asking for favours, and having none to give in return, while the Member can often forget party completely, and boast with justification that he is at the service of all his constituents. It would never occur to him to inquire whether one of them who came to him for help had supported him or not at the previous election. The candidate would be wise to anticipate the neutral, paternal attitude of the Member, by disengaging himself as often as he can from the purely party aspect of his work. If he places the emphasis on winning support for himself, or, more modestly, for his party, he will rapidly bore his electors. Let his ultimate intention be self-evident in the trouble he takes to familiarize himself with his constituency. When he goes to a works-canteen or a dairy-farm, he should go as the person who may suddenly be called upon in the next two or three years to speak with authority on their behalf, not as the person who is anxious to secure their votes. The second object is implicit in the first, but they will be more likely to vote for him if they think he cares more for them than for himself.

For the same reason, a representative, potential or actual, should involve himself as much as possible in the non-political life of his constituency, which amounts to nine-tenths of the interests and activities of the people who live there. A politician is not like a doctor or sanitary inspector, who are concerned with only one aspect of people's lives. He is concerned with all, for there is almost nothing which can happen to anybody which in one form or another may not be a proper subject for Parliament to discuss. So, having this excuse to go everywhere, it is much to his advantage to make use of it. As an invited or self-invited guest to the amateur dramatic society, the village gymkhana or the Rotarian luncheon, he is not intruding politics into other people's pleasures, but allowing other people's pleasures to fertilize his politics.

All this will take time. He may resent the erosion of the little leisure left to him by attendance at the House, and say with Burke, when his constituents reproached him with the rareness of his appearances: 'But, gentlemen, I live a hundred miles distance from Bristol; and at the end of a session I come to my own house, fatigued in body and mind, to a little repose, and to a very little attention to my family and private concerns. . . . I could hardly serve you as I have done, and court you too.' He did not convince them. Nor will the modern back-bench Member, with fifty times Burke's electorate, and a tenth of his genius. He must court his electors constantly, and the methods of his courtship are approachability and service.

I have sketched an ideal portrait of a Member's relationship with his constituents to show how little party orthodoxy or political acumen may count in comparison with those more human qualities which cause one man to be liked and the next disliked. If a Member or candidate has revealed himself to his constituents as austere and forbidding, there is nothing to cushion the shock if a clash eventually comes between him and them on an issue of political principle. If, on a single occasion, he has left a supporter humiliated in argument or ignored in a chance encounter, the incident will be remembered and recounted against him, and unpopularity due to such trivial, often unrealized, causes can spread with alarming speed. In reverse, a local reputation for accessibility, charm of manner, conscientiousness, and a sense of humour, is a priceless basis on which to found a political career. In such cases unorthodoxy can be an additional merit in the eyes of those whose hearts have already been won. In our own day, Sir Robert Boothby is the best example of it. The British public like a buccaneer: they enjoy pugnacity. They dislike pretension, irritability, aloofness, and unorthodoxy without the personality to sustain it.

Reputation, and the qualities which create it, are put to the test most dramatically at a General Election. Every Member of Parliament dreads an election; every prospective candidate longs for it. For one it may be the end; for the other, the beginning. But for the local party workers it is the culmination of their efforts, the one moment when their devotion is rewarded by a sense of importance, and when their Member, stripped temporarily of his membership, becomes wholly their own. Each election is a new honeymoon between them. Even if they have fought for years a losing battle against an entrenched majority, and expect in their hearts to lose again, their candidate is at least a runner with an outside chance. This sporting element in a General Election, which becomes a Derby in which every person can back his favourite stable and his own locality is allotted a particular horse from it, is of far greater importance than the discussion of the rival policies. Ninety per cent of the votes are decided before the argument starts, and those whose prime business it is to swing the remaining 10 per cent in their party's favour, would feel as insulted by a suggestion that they might themselves form part of the 10 per cent, as a regimental officer by the suggestion that he might desert. It is during the election campaign that party loyalty becomes elevated to a major virtue, and so intense is the emotion generated in those three weeks, that it colours a person's whole political attitude during the four or five subsequent years. The standard-bearer of their battalion, their parliamentary candidate, is the personification of the party. Whether they like or dislike him personally, once adopted, he *is* the party. If they can strive so hard for his success, it seems inconceivable at that moment that he would ever do other than give to the party's leader the same unwavering support as they have given to him.

The purpose of the party manager at the centre is to create a national image of the party which will not vary from constituency to constituency. 'He hopes that whenever the name of his organization is heard, there shall follow, as day follows night, a chain of affective associations—honourable record, wise policies, just aims, powerful leaders.'[1] It is his intention that the same arguments, pledges and criticisms shall simultaneously be presented from every platform in the country. A stream of daily notes, transcripts of key speeches by the party's spokesmen and sample answers to questionnaires, issue from the central offices to each candidate throughout the campaign. The simplest image to create is that of the leader. His face beams down from every hoarding; it is seen three or four times in as many weeks on the television screens; his name is the button which, when pressed, causes a nightly buzz of approval in a thousand halls. The candi-

[1] Mark Benney, *How People Vote*. London, 1956, p. 75.

date is merely the leader's local alias. He is assumed, quite properly, to be his mouthpiece, and as mouthpieces have tongues, but not minds, of their own, the party orthodoxy of the candidate is not a convenience merely, but a necessity, a virtue. Individual glosses on party policy are confusing and even dangerous, and the candidate who makes reservations, or introduces into his speeches or election address a note of warning that he holds strong personal views on subjects which may arise during the next Parliament, on capital punishment, for instance, or on the Free Trade Area, is not likely to be praised for his candour, but blamed for his clumsiness. It only puzzles and dismays his supporters.

The time has surely come for party managers and candidates to seek new methods of approach to an educated electorate. They would hotly protest that it is not their purpose to use all modern means of mass-communication to create a mass mind which does not require to think and therefore ceases to discriminate, yet this is precisely the effect of party management today. They are sub-consciously echoing the sentiments expressed by Senator Alexander Wiley when there was a glut of cheese in the United States: 'Our problem is not too much cheese produced, but rather too little cheese consumed.' But politics is not a monster job of advertising and public relations. It is a public debate on great issues. Bryce's definition, made in 1888, still aptly describes what ought to happen: 'A General Election in England is an expression of popular opinion on the two or three leading measures then pro-pounded and discussed by the party leaders, as well as a vote of confidence or no confidence in the Ministry of the day.' Since he wrote, it might have been imagined that radio, television, popular newspapers and general education would have facilitated the process of discovering, instructing and expressing the public's point-of-view. But they have merely served to stamp it out from two huge rounded moulds. The chain of Liberal successes and near-successes during by-elections in the winter and spring of 1958 was not so much a protest against the policies of the two great parties, as against the contemptuous assumption that political opinion can be organized by the same methods as a taste for cheese.

But this is an inter-election attitude. At by-elections an individual candidate can make an impact on the electorate, and an individual elector feels relatively free to protest. At General Elections the people are choosing a Government and not a Member of Parliament. They return to their old loyalties, and surrender to the embraces of the mother-party which at other moments they find stifling.

I look back on my own past election-addresses with shame. I did no more than ladle out to my electorate a bowl of soup from the party tureen. I wrote nothing which I did not, and still do not believe, but my addresses were deliberately depersonalized. I left out whatever I feared might be unexpected or might prove inconvenient. An election address should express a personal attitude, not a complete party programme. There will be time, even too much time, to expound the programme verbally during the campaign, and the electors can scarcely open a newspaper without discovering what it is. The candidate should do all he can to reveal himself as an individual; a supporter, but not a blurred carbon copy, of his leader. If, here and there, he disagrees, it will not weaken his chances if he declares his disagreement. His workers will soon discover that it is not something that they need explain away.

Similarly, he should remind the public that an election is not a two-barrelled shot-gun discharged at quinquennial intervals in their faces, but a debate in which they have the major part to play. Too often, an election takes the form of a state-trial, with the Government spokesman as the prisoner in the dock conducting his own defence; the Opposition as counsel for the prosecution; and the electors as the jury. This is a misconception of all three roles. The electors have a duty to intervene in the argument, not merely to give their verdict when it is over. They cannot do this effectively if their local candidate is by the rules of the game unable to modify his party's views in accordance with his own firmly held convictions or to meet an opinion strongly expressed to him by his electors; or if the electors remain at home by their unresponsive television sets, and never attend his meetings. Of course there must be general agreement between candidate and leader, between candidate and supporters. I am only pleading for greater elasticity in the attitude permitted to him on particular issues, greater participation by the electors, and less insistence by the party headquarters that a difference of opinion is a matter for regret and shame. This monolithic attitude does not exist within parliamentary parties once they are elected; why should it exist during the process of election, at the one moment when reasonable diversity of opinion can be most fruitful?

It is not as if a party was binding itself in detail by its election programme. If it did so, it would be wrong on two counts. First because it would be unreasonable to expect the public to be good judges of legislative proposals. 'The best the public can do,' wrote A. F. Pollard, 'is to judge of the work done in its service, without attempting to do the work of its servants'; and even the Webbs thought that the only proper function of the people is to 'assent to results'. Secondly, a Parliament can last five years, and what might seem right or desirable in the election year, might be wrong or impracticable as little as a year later. To encourage the people to demand details would be to convert an election into an auction. 'I bid 5/- on the retirement pension,' one candidate would say. 'I'll make it 7/6d,' replies his fellow. Already one often hears the cry from the back of the hall, 'What's your policy?' by which the heckler means, 'What are your promises?' At the time it may seem unreasonable and lame to side-step the question, but the candidate is foolish if he does not answer in terms of general principle only. To do so puts him, except momentarily, in the strongest possible position. When unforeseeable events occur during the subsequent parliament, he is not only free of embarrassing pledges, but he is able to relate his views on the new situation to the principles for which he asked his electors' support. If he can show complete consistency between the two, his moral and political position is unchallengeable. Finally, such an attitude is a constant reminder to his constituents of what an election is for, and of the real difference between a representative and a delegate.

I have said that the passionate loyalty to a party and its leader induced by a General Election colours the attitude of keen party-workers during the whole period between elections. The same is true, to an only slightly less extent, of the party conference. I cannot believe that there are many political leaders, particularly in the Conservative Party, who actually enjoy the conference. It is one of the major shoals through which they have to steer the party during its annual course down the river. The passage is not easy, but if safely navigated, the barque is carried onwards at a greater rate, and the experience is stimulating, if frightening, to the captain and his chief lieutenants. But to those who attend as representatives of their constituency parties, the conference is the political event of the year to which they most look forward. They meet their leaders, not only in the conference, but socially at the many receptions organized for their benefit; they meet each other in an atmosphere which combines pleasure with the excuse of work; and they are flattered by the fiction that they are there to make policy at the summit.

In fact, in neither of the major parties, does the conference have power of final decision. The difference between them is that in the Conservative Party theory coincides with practice; in the Labour Party the fiction is maintained in spite of practice. The difference in theory is well illustrated by comparing Mr Attlee's definition of the function of his party's conference with Lord Kilmuir's definition of his. Mr Attlee said: 'The Labour Party conference lays down the policy of the party, and issues instructions which must be carried out by the Executive, the affiliated organizations and its representatives in Parliament and on local authorities.'[1] Lord Kilmuir (as Sir David Maxwell-Fyfe) declared: 'The Leader is served by the party's various policy committees, and these in their turn are influenced by the views of the party as revealed in the various resolutions at the party conference. . . . But endorsements and pronouncements on party policy are the prerogative and responsibility of the Leader.'[2]

Attempts have often been made by the Conservative Party's opponents to ridicule this uncompromising doctrine. The term 'Leader', with its unhappy continental echoes; his non-appearance at the conference debates until they are technically completed; the remote 'influence' which the views expressed at the conference are allowed to have upon his decisions: all these, in Socialist eyes, add up to grossly undemocratic practice. If they choose to search

[1] C. R. Attlee, *The Labour Party in Perspective*. London, 1949, p. 78.
[2] *Report on Party Organization*. 1949.

the records as assiduously as Mr R. T. McKenzie has done, they
could find evidence to support their claim. Mr McKenzie could
quote only one example, the famous resolution on 300,000 houses
at the 1950 conference, where a conference vote had the direct
result of reversing party policy,[1] and even in this case, it could be
said that the resolution only applied a touch of the whip to a not
too reluctant horse. But, of course, resolutions are not ineffective
because they are not accepted *in toto*, and most of them are anticipated in framing party policy, just because the leaders are well
aware of the mood of their supporters in the country, and are
anxious to avoid a clash. It has never happened, for instance,
that a Conservative leader, having gained his point in Parliament, has subsequently been disowned by his party at its annual
conference.

The Labour Party, owing to the fiction which Mr Attlee
reaffirmed so bluntly, and because of the structure of its conference,
risks almost every year a dangerous rocking of the boat. Since the
Parliamentary Labour Party emerged out of the Trades Unions
and an existing national party, it is still, so to speak, the junior
partner. It must watch very carefully the movement of opinion
within the Unions, which collectively control five-sixths of the
conference's voting strength. But Labour's parliamentary leaders
have shown consistent courage in standing up for their own
opinions. On minor points they have actually ignored conference decisions, such as the resolution to abolish tied cottages,
which was passed in two successive years, 1947 and 1948; and
on major matters, like German rearmament in 1954 and the
hydrogen bomb in 1957, they have risked defeat, the consequences
of which would have been incalculable.

McKenzie sums up his admirable analysis (from which many
of the foregoing examples are derived) in this way: 'The mass
organizations can and do exact a certain price for their labour; they
expect to be listened to by their leaders. Like Bagehot's constitutional monarch, the annual party conference has the right to
be consulted, the right to encourage, and the right to warn. But
this is not to say that the members of the mass organization have
the right to control or direct the actions of their parliamentary

[1] R. T. McKenzie, *British Political Parties*. London, 1955, p. 221.

leaders.'[1] They obtain their greatest satisfaction simply from being there.

In neither party is it quite clear whether they are there as representatives or as delegates of their local parties. The former is the more flattering term, and it coincides with the wishes of the platform, for delegates with mandated votes are *ipso facto* immune to new arguments. Nor, in my experience, is it their wish to be entrusted with more power. They enjoy the fiction, the appearance, of power without its responsibilities. One of the strangest aspects of a great party conference is the audience's capacity to swing, often in the space of a few minutes, between militancy and deference. They seem tacitly to accept Lord Snowden's judgement, 'There is all the difference in the world between the licence and irresponsibility of a conference, and the position of a Government which has to face practical difficulties and knows that no Government can move far ahead of public opinion.'[2] The loudly applauded hyperbole of speeches on the cost of living and the Trades Unions at recent Conservative conferences were not reflected in the subsequent votes. A reply by a respected Minister can extinguish passion as easily as a lightning-conductor. The fact of having made or cheered inflammatory speeches in the presence of the party leaders is itself amply satisfying, and Sir Norman Angell's fear that 'the rash and responsible leader is apt to be edged out by the leader who promises action',[3] is not borne out in practice. The conferences arouse almost messianic zeal, which is not always pleasant to witness, but their lasting effect is more on the emotions than on policy.

An election is the period of closest co-operation between a Member and his party workers, for only then is he divorced from Parliament and from all his constituents who are not also his supporters. At a party conference he is not, unless a Minister or potential Minister, expected to take the centre of the stage. If too many back-bench Members mount the rostrum, there is audible

[1] McKenzie, p. 583.
[2] Philip Snowden, *An Autobiography*. Vol. 1, p. 87.
[3] *Sunday Times*, September 8th, 1957.

resentment. But taken together, election and conference give the party its character and unity. It is too easily assumed that because of their shared emotion and experience on these two occasions, both Members and workers will regard the party from the same point of view. In this fallacy lies trouble. They don't.

The Member is not caught up in mass-emotion. He knows too well the tricks by which it can be created. Those god-like Ministers on the platform are men whom he sees daily, of whom he may even be contemptuous or jealous. He does not enjoy undiluted adulation, and dislikes party conferences for the same reason as he would dislike speaking in the House of Commons to empty benches opposite. An election fills a Member, or all but few of them, with loathing. He is obliged to mask the qualifications with which he would normally clothe his naked party arguments. He is in a false position, and only the excitement of the campaign, the constant pressure of work, the hope of victory, the sense of responsibility to friends and helpers, enable him to assume during those three weeks a personality alien to his own.

When the election is over, a light curtain drops once more between the Member and his party-workers. For most of the time he is away at Westminster, from which constant publicity has not yet been able to tear the veil of faint mystery, and when he visits the constituency, he is slightly more than life-size, and belongs to all, not to the handful who laboured so hard for his success. While they are still party-men, he is not exclusively a party-man. In his self-estimation, he is elected to watch his own party as closely as the opposition. He is one of the several guardians of the policy which he expounded and his supporters endorsed, and guardianship must sometimes involve the duty to criticize, and to expose heresy as he conceives it. But his dual role of party-man and party-critic is one which has not always found acceptance, for it can easily be made to appear contradictory. Little difficulty arises when the party-voters themselves feel dissatisfied by their party's policy or its presentation: there is no inconsistency for them in grumbling about the cost of living or the policy of the hydrogen bomb and continuing to give the party their support, since they have little responsibility and they know that individually their protests carry little weight. But when the Member expresses equivalent misgivings which some of his supporters do not happen to share, doubt is thrown by them on his loyalty and integrity, even though he may at that moment be living up to those two qualities more fully than he ever has before. To what extent are they justified in bringing pressure on him to force him to change his mind?

The dilemma has long been recognized, but never solved. In the last chapter of this book I shall suggest a basis for a solution. Here I am only concerned with current precept and practice, and the ways in which conflict between the Member and his constituency party-supporters can arise, owing to their basically different attitudes to the party-system.

Parliament itself has little to say on the matter, for Parliament recognizes party to so small an extent that no record of a Member's party appears in any official publication of the House, including Hansard and the division lists. The Committee of Privileges stated in 1947 that 'it is a breach of privilege to take or to threaten action which is not merely calculated to threaten the Member's course of action in Parliament, but is of a kind against which it is absolutely necessary that Members should be protected if they are to discharge their duties as such independently and without fear of punishment or hope of reward.' But they were referring not to constituency party pressure, but to the threat of a Union to withdraw financial support from their spokesman in Parliament, Mr W. J. Brown, if he did not speak and vote in accordance with their wishes. The right of a constituent to threaten to withdraw support from his Member if he did not vote in a certain way, was firmly upheld by the Speaker in 1946. Mr Hector Hughes had raised, as a matter of privilege, a telegram from a constituent which read: 'Cannot continue support if you encourage Transport Bill. *A King, 2 Rosehill Avenue, Aberdeen.*' 'Anybody, surely,' replied the Speaker, to murmurs of approval from the House, 'can write to his Member and say, "Look here, if you vote for this, I will not support you at the next Election." That is not intimidation.'[1] Erskine May records other instances where it has been held to be a breach of privilege to challenge a Member to fight a duel, publish a poster containing a threat to him, and even

[1] *Hansard*, vol. 431, col. 1968. December 18th, 1946.

to write him a letter about cruel sports threatening to inform his constituents, if no answer was received, that their Member had no objection to cruelty to animals. But, in general, Members must pay as much or as little heed to constituency pressure as they think fit. They will obtain no protection from an imaginary law of the constitution.

The protection they obtain from the party headquarters is limited to broad statements of principle, which constituency Associations are invited to implement. The official Conservative pamphlet which deals with the adoption of candidates quotes Burke's famous words:

Your representative owes you not his industry only, but his judgement; and he betrays, instead of serving you, if he sacrifices it to your opinion . . . . Authoritative instructions, mandates issued, which the Member is bound blindly and implicitly to obey, to vote, and to argue for, though contrary to the clearest conviction of his judgement and conscience—these are things utterly unknown to the laws of this land, and which arise from a fundamental mistake of the whole order and tenor of our constitution. . . . You choose a member indeed; but when you have chosen him, he is not member of Bristol, but he is a member of Parliament.[1]

In the great majority of cases, this solemn reminder is enough to deter a constituency Association from lashing out at their Member in sudden anger. If he disgraces himself and his party by his personal behaviour, that is, of course, another matter. An Association cannot continue to support a man who has been found guilty of drunkenness in charge of a car, or has involved himself in a discreditable affair with one of his constituents' wives. If he becomes too old, or is too obviously inefficient to do his job, and refuses to take a hint, then he must be gently but firmly eased out of his seat. If it is a question of persistent disagreement with the party on fundamental points of principle, then again there is every reason for the Association to indicate to the Member that he is unlikely to be readopted at the next election.

All these cases are comparatively simple. The difficulty arises when a Conservative Association quarrels with the Member on

[1] Edmund Burke, *Speech at the Conclusion of the Poll.* 1774. Beaconsfield Edition. Vol. II, pp. 95-6.

two or three political issues spread over a number of years. Should the local party then threaten him with expulsion unless he mends his ways? If they do not, they are saddled with a Member whom many of them do not trust. If they do, they are ignoring Burke's law, and defying the precepts of their party leaders. Of one thing they can be quite certain, that the decision will be left to them. Central Office will not interfere. However esteemed the Member may be by his party leaders or his colleagues in the House, he depends for his seat on the goodwill, and on the subscriptions and hard work, of his voluntary workers in the constituency. If he offends them by opposing his party, he must discuss the matter with them beforehand, and afterwards make the best case he can for acting as he did. If he fails to persuade a majority, and if the final decision is come to after as much time as possible has been given to considering it, and without resort to calumny or other discreditable tactics, then he must accept his dismissal.

One further qualification is necessary: 'a majority' means a majority of members of the Association. It does not mean, at one extreme, a majority of his Executive Council, which consists, perhaps, of no more than fifty persons out of thirty thousand local Conservative voters; nor, at the other extreme, of the whole thirty thousand, only a minority of whom are identifiable. Should such a situation arise, the Member will obviously attempt to persuade every *bona fide* local Conservative who supports him to qualify for a vote by joining the Association. Though constitutionally he cannot be prevented from putting his case to the test of an independent candidature at the election, he would be acting more in the spirit of the party's traditions if he faces his Association squarely, argues the case on the merits of the action he took and its consistency with membership of the parliamentary party, allows passions to cool, and then accepts their final verdict. To stand as an Independent against an official Conservative candidate chosen to replace him will risk the loss of the seat. To thousands of Conservatives, who have never heard of Burke and are not greatly concerned with theoretical issues, but simply wish to vote for their party at an election which may be critical, it would seem unpardonable for the ousted Member to split an established majority. To him it might appear an act of principle; to them it would be an act of selfishness and spite. Even if he were to win, his triumph would be a form of fratricide, and the feud would be likely to continue throughout the life of the succeeding Parliament. The Association is open to all who support the party. If after careful consideration a majority of them show that their Member has lost their confidence, whether he thinks them right or wrong in their opinion, he is no less a casualty of the democratic process than if he lost his seat at the General Election itself.

I have stated what I believe to be the present attitude of the Conservative Party on serious breaches between an Association and its Member. I agree with it except in a single particular. I believe that if the Chairman of the party feels that an Association has acted with unnecessary hastiness against their Member, he should state his views publicly. To do so is to risk the protest that the autonomy rule was being violated: but not to do so is to risk the more serious accusation that his silence implies consent. The whole party could thus become the scape-goat for the impetuosity of a single Association. What is the purpose of a code of conduct if no comment can be made upon an infringement of its spirit, but only of its letter? Such cases occur so rarely that there is danger that the code itself may be forgotten, and a single reprimand would be the best means of preventing a recurrence. When these situations arise they attract public attention far outside the constituency, and the party's reputation is needlessly endangered.

There can be terrible consequences for Parliament and for the whole nation if constituencies use their privileges in a spasm of sudden anger to crush independent thought and action in Parliament. These words, for example, need no comment; they were spoken by the chairman of the Chigwell branch of the Epping Conservative Association in March, 1939:

Mr Churchill's post-Munich insurrection was shocking. His castigation of the National Government, which we return him to support, would, in any other party but the Conservative Party, have earned him immediate expulsion. Loyal Conservatives in the Epping Division have been placed in an intolerable position. I feel that unless Mr Churchill is prepared to work for the National Government and the Prime Minister, he ought no longer to shelter under the goodwill and name of such a great party.[1]

The chairman of the Chigwell branch was no political nonentity. He now sits on the Conservative benches of the House of Commons.

[1] Quoted by Roger Fulford in his *Ramsay Muir Memorial Lecture*. Oxford, 1957

Chapter Three

THE MEMBER IN PARLIAMENT

The revealing power of the House of Commons—the party battle at Westminster —complexity of parliamentary business—temptation to laziness—'sheep-like' voting—external pressures on a Member—constituency letters—is he his constituency's advocate?—national pressure-groups—a Member's connection with business interests or Trades Union—pressure from party headquarters— free votes—back-bench pressure on Ministers—party-loyalty in Parliament— function of the Whips—party-committees—differences between the two major parties—the Labour Party's 'conscience clause'—which parliamentary party is the more tolerant?—Lord Hailsham on independence of judgement

AS I FIRST stood at the bar of the House, on February 19th, 1952, ready to take my seat after a by-election which had aroused no more than ordinary interest, a senior Member whispered in my ear, 'In a few minutes you will walk behind the Speaker's chair into the obscurity from which you should probably never have emerged.' It was my first lesson in parliamentary deflation. To come from the concentrated arc-lights, the excitement, the triumph, of an election, to the goal of your ambition, and find that the size of your majority is better known than your name, is an immediate reminder that you are of so little significance that when you die or lose your seat, you will probably be replaced as easily as a broken window-pane.

It is historical continuity which has made Parliament greater than the sum of all its ephemeral members. Reading the reports of debates two hundred years old, it is possible to recapture exactly the mood of the House on that particular day. The forms of speech, the interruptions, the procedure, the very character of individual Members, are as authentically reproduced in our own time as the chimes of an eighteenth-century clock. But it is not only the antiquity of Parliament which cuts a man down in size. It is its terrible power to sum up character and detect fraud. Like a television camera, Parliament catches him at his weakest and most exposed. Even David Lloyd-George confessed that he could not rise to his feet at the dispatch box without his knees knocking together. It is in part due to the shape of the Chamber, which ensures that the speaker will have his back turned to his friends and face the concentrated glare of his opponents, but also to the knowledge that he only has an audience because all the other Members present are waiting for him to sit down so that they will have a chance to talk themselves. After trying for six hours to catch the Speaker's eye to deliver a speech already whittled down by the speeches of others, the Member begins to wonder why he exposes himself to the ordeal. The humiliating, enervating, revealing power of Parliament is in these moments at its most merciless.

Constituents, when they speak of Parliament as a talking shop ('Why don't you *do* something?'), can have little idea of the hypnotic power it exerts. All its members are linked by common experience of its disappointments, of how far achievement in debate lags behind intention. 'I do not think I know any bores in the House,' wrote Lord Wedgwood with some audacity, 'so well are we trained to confine self-advertisement to the Chamber and our constituencies. . . . Inside the House, that bitterness of party strife outside, to which we have to conform in public, strikes us as somewhat vulgar.'[1] It is one of the few places where the bore is forced to recognize himself as such, and one of the marks of a parliamentary bore is to allow his political attitude to affect his personal relationships. The violence of the controversy in the Chamber is at least in part a show. It will not be reproduced in any other quarter of the House, and the printed record of debates gives but the faintest hint of the underlying unity. Politicians, the creators of party, are often the most appalled by their own creation. All of them enjoy an occasional row and the dexterity with which the sabres are handled by their champions. But this is one of the manifestations of Parliament, not its object. Its greatest failure is not to have made the distinction evident to the world outside.

Parliament also teaches its Members, as it never can the public, that government is immensely complex, and that a clear mind for administration is as important a qualification for membership as strong political conviction. Two-thirds of the time of Parliament is spent in discussing what is possible: the other third is spent in discussing what is desirable. In the constituencies the proportions

[1] Lord Wedgwood, *Testament to Democracy*. London, 1942, p. 17.

are generally reversed. Constant, though indirect, contact with members of the civil service, who from their box under the gallery must so often regard their legislators in the same light as the legislators regard their constituents, gradually eliminates a man's contempt for careful forethought, teaches him the difference between an exception and a precedent, and warns him when a fire will burn itself out and when to call the fire-brigade. He soon begins to realize that decisions of government are usually right, even though most of his attention is concentrated on the occasions when they may be wrong. He comes to admit to himself, though he may continue to say the opposite, that some grievances are incapable of solution except by creating other grievances ten times as bad.

Parliament is not dull. How can it be dull when almost every facet of the nation's life and work comes up sooner or later for debate, and when daily a Member associates with men who have immense power in their hands? There is no need for him to attend the debates which bore him. The libraries and dining rooms are among the best-stocked and most comfortable in London, and if occasionally the House is a prison for an evening or a night, it is a prison from which no visitors are barred. The variety of business, the constant heightening and lowering of tension, the plotting, planning and grouping of men and women who have learned to tolerate the few of their colleagues whom they do not respect, dispel the weariness which is popularly supposed to overcome every Member in his sixth or seventh year. It is not so much boredom which robs him of his early enthusiasm, as unfulfilled ambition or laziness.

On my first day in Parliament, Mr Hugh Dalton said to me, 'This is the most competitive place in the world. If you are modest, everyone will like you. If you are ambitious, and look like succeeding, people will become jealous.' That may be true; I am in no position to judge. But I am acutely aware of the temptation to be lazy. It is too easy to give others, and even oneself, the impression of ceaseless activity, while accomplishing nothing. A whole day can agreeably disappear in answering half-a-dozen constituency letters in the morning while attending a Standing Committee with only a quarter-ear open to the debate, listening to

Questions and Ministerial statements from 2.30 to 4 p.m., looking in on two party committees in the evening, entertaining a couple of visiting Americans to drinks on the terrace, and then gossiping in the Smoking Room till it is time for bed. The fact that twelve hours have been spent in his place of work, and that many constituents will begin their letters with the words, 'I hesitate to trouble you when I know that you are so tremendously busy,' is flattering to a Member's self-esteem. There is no place where a man can occupy himself more intensively or usefully, and no place where he can hold down his job by doing so little. The very magnitude and variety of the business that comes before Parliament are deterrents to hard work. There is too much to absorb it all; why try to absorb any? And then modesty, false or real, creeps in as an excuse: 'What have I to contribute on this subject? Who wants to listen to me, when so-and-so is here with his immense knowledge and experience? In any case, the subject is of no possible interest to my constituents. I'll listen to the opening speeches, and then have tea.'

Indolence is one of the by-products of party discipline. A Member can win a certain amount of commendation by saying nothing, even listening to nothing, but simply by voting in the right lobby when required. Docility will not carry him to the front bench, but it will content his constituents and provide for himself a calm passage through the parliamentary year. Moreover, in supplying a dependable and constantly available vote, such a Member is contributing to the stability of government. This is what Christopher Hollis meant by his paradox, 'The world has been saved again and again by the laziness of its politicians',[1] but later in his book, he exploded with indignation at the system: 'As things are now,' he wrote,' 'it would really be simpler and more economical to keep a flock of tame sheep and from time to time to drive them through the division lobbies in the appropriate numbers.' Winston Churchill has said much the same thing: 'The earnest party man becomes a silent drudge, tramping at intervals through lobbies to record his vote, and wondering why he comes to Westminster at all.'[2] The criticism is repeated almost

[1] Christopher Hollis, *Can Parliament Survive?* London, 1949, p. 36.
[2] Winston Churchill, *Life of Lord Randolph Churchill.* Vol. I, p. 69.

daily, often by the same person who would protest most loudly if his Member strayed.

A Member is subjected to many forms of pressure to steer him into the right or the 'wrong' lobby, and the main purpose of this chapter is to indicate their relative strength. They can roughly be divided into two groups: pressures from outside Parliament, including pressure from his constituents, his party headquarters, his Trades Union or business associates, his personal friends, and national organizations; and pressures from inside Parliament, including his colleagues, his Whips, his Ministers or shadow-Cabinet, and his party-committees. The resultant of this parallelogram of forces is almost always the same: he votes as he is required to vote by his Whips. But the reasons why he does so, and what can be the different methods and consequences of not doing so, are not so simple.

Pressure from the constituency is not the same as pressure from the local constituency party, which was discussed in the last chapter. It can include pressure from the opposite party, sometimes from its prospective candidate himself; from individuals who write without declaring their politics; and from a multitude of local bodies ranging from the Council, the Church, and the Chamber of Trade to a village bowling club. If like Peel, Members feel 'perfectly careless of the opinions which prevail out of doors', it would be folly for them to say so: in fact, they often devote more care to answering such letters politely and reasonably than they do to the current business of Parliament itself.

Members distinguish between appeals from an individual constituent for action in his personal interests, and appeals from an organization for action on behalf of local interests as a whole. In the former case, no conflict arises: an attempt is made to persuade the Minister to grant the request, either by private letter, or by personal approach, or, in the last resort, by raising the matter publicly on the Adjournment. If the attempt fails, the reasons why it failed should be given in detail to the constituent, for his right to an explanation of government actions which affect him directly is as basic as his right to protest against them. If a Member considers that such a protest is wholly unreasonable, he should, in my opinion, spare his Minister the trouble of investigating it, for the

Member is not only a link between people and Executive: he is also a sieve.

More difficult is the proper attitude for a Member to adopt towards his local authority when it asks him to take action in Parliament on lines which he or his party strongly disapproves. Should he act as counsel for his constituency and accept the brief, or refuse to argue a case which he thinks unsound? If it concerns the constituency alone, or a small group of authorities of which his own is one, he cannot refuse. It would be intolerable if another Member had to be found to present a Corporation's Private Bill, or if the sitting Member argued publicly against his constituency's special interests. At those moments, he is an advocate pure and simple, and the House recognizes him as such. But if conflicting national issues are involved, then he must not allow himself to be swept away by local patriotism. Let me give two examples: I have pleaded consistently in Parliament that the cost of protecting the coast-line against erosion should be made a national charge on the Exchequer, knowing that if I were the Member for Coventry, I would probably argue that coast protection should fall mainly on the rates of the coastal resorts. On the other hand, I thought it wrong to press for a special allocation of steel to rebuild one of Bournemouth's piers at a time when steel was in short supply: if I had done so, I might have gained a little local popularity, but I would momentarily have embarrassed the Government without helping my constituents, and I would have drawn uselessly upon the small reservoir of credit which each Member hopes to keep at the Ministry of Housing and Local Government.

Any national body which seeks to bring pressure on Members of Parliament will be more likely to succeed if it organizes the campaign on a constituency-Member basis. Roneos addressed and posted from a London headquarters have only one destination, the waste-paper basket. But a letter written in personal terms from the local branch of the society will certainly be read and almost as certainly answered. It forces the Member to take the campaign seriously. Here is some more advice for campaign promoters: stamp the letter with a 3d stamp, post it to arrive on the Thursday morning before the relevant debate, put the essence of the case in a very short covering letter and enclose an expanded statement of the argument, find out which Members have a special interest in the subject (ten well-aimed letters are better than 630 circulars), interview the Secretaries of the two relevant party committees, and persuade local branches with Members on your select list to seek interviews with them in their constituencies. How often is this advice disregarded! Identically worded post-cards arrive in shoals and set up in Members a counter-feeling of irritation. They immediately arouse the suspicion, as Mr Stewart has aptly put it, that their purpose 'is not so much to indicate opinion as to simulate it'.[1] Such campaigns cannot be disregarded; they usually manage to fill the House half-full on a Friday afternoon. But they are rarely successful, for the reasons which Mr Michael Astor well expressed in the debate on the Sunday opening of the Festival of Britain Fun Fair: 'A minority faction, particularly in matters of religion, is always the most active and most noisy in putting forward its case. By and large, it is the person who may take a more tolerant and lenient view, and who feels himself to be in a majority, who does not express his point of view. . . . Unless we take a stand, these societies may exert in the House in terms of legislation, an influence out of all proportion to their representation in the country.'[2] It is a strange fact that the most direct and traditional approach of elector to Member, by lobbying him on some specific issue of national policy, is one of the least effective.

One of the least recognized forms of pressure on a Member is that of his friends and professional associates. The House of Commons is among the most uncorrupt assemblies in the world, if for no other reason than that the risks of exposure are infinitely greater than the possible rewards. The disclosures of the Lynskey Tribunal and the few instances of Budget leaks, are fresh in everybody's mind because of their rarity. When occasionally the relationships between politicians and outside financial interests have been revealed in merciless detail, as by the Bank Rate Tribunal in 1957–8, the probity of politicians has been demonstrated beyond question. I know of a few Members who claim to have been offered bribes, and the combination of amusement

---

[1] J. D. Stewart, *British Pressure Groups: their role in relation to the House of Commons.* Oxford, 1958.

[2] *Hansard,* vol. 481, col. 585. November 23rd, 1950.

and disgust with which such offers have been rejected is itself the best guarantee against their repetition. As is well known, it is the practice of the House that a Member shall declare any financial interest he has in the subject at the beginning of his speech, and the House is left to balance the greater authority which such interests lend to his words against the possibility of special pleading. It would be absurd to prevent a man from contributing his inside knowledge of an industry on the ground that he might influence policy in its favour. The national interest can be quite consistent with advocacy of the special interests with which he openly identifies himself.

It is the same with a Labour Member's connection with a Trades Union. Perhaps the Union has paid the bulk of his election expenses, or even an annual retainer as long as he stays in Parliament. In such circumstances he would obviously not speak against the Union's interests. But then he would not do so in any case, paid or not paid. A life-time of service to the Union outside Parliament would make him a devoted servant of the Union inside. If a Conservative were to say that mine-workers were grossly overpaid, it would be as instinctive for an ex-miner on the opposite benches to jump up and protest, as it would be for Major Legge-Bourke to react against a Socialist attack on the Brigade of Guards. Nor would a Trades Union Member find it obligatory on him to execute the instructions of his Union if he disagreed with them. He would argue the matter out in private, and in his speech to the House present the highest common factor of agreement. If he did not do so, it would soon become obvious to his colleagues, and eventually to the House as a whole, that he was nothing but a hack, and he would lose any influence he might have had. The strongest deterrent against any form of subservience to outside interests is fear of exposure and ridicule.

Influence by a party headquarters is on the borderline between external and internal pressures, because in both major parties many of the same individuals are in ultimate control of the party in Parliament and of the party in the country. In the Conservative Party, indeed, pressure by Central Office does not exist at all. It is conceivable that the Party Chairman might privately advise a back-bench Member for or against a certain line of action, and point out to him the likely effects of dissent on the party as a whole; but today it would be hard to say whether he would be speaking as Chairman of the party or as a senior member of the Cabinet. Conservatives look on their Central Office as a propaganda machine, the organizer of conferences, a rallying-point for party-agents, a clearing-house of speakers and candidates, and a useful source of political information, but never as a dictator of policy. Years might elapse without a Conservative Member receiving a single communication from Central Office except an occasional request to address a meeting and copies of their current publications.

In the Labour Party, the situation is complicated by the interposition of the National Executive Committee, which has no exact parallel in the Conservative Party. The NEC, a body with twenty-seven members, twelve of whom are Trades Unionists, has the right, not infrequently used, to disown a Member and even to disaffiliate his constituency Labour Party. It is therefore an extra-parliamentary power with which an intending Socialist rebel has to contend. But although in theory the NEC is the governing body of the whole Labour movement between conferences, in practice Mr Attlee and his successors have managed to keep policy-making in the hands of the leaders in Parliament. This is partly because it would be thought intolerable under the British constitution if an outside party organization could dictate to a Government in detail what it should do; and partly because, even when in opposition, the leaders of the parliamentary party are regarded by the other members of the NEC with 'mingled awe and respect'.[1] One of the few who attempted to take a line of his own was Harold Laski. As Chairman of the Labour Party in the summer of 1946, he brought down on his head Mr Attlee's classic snub: 'You have no right whatever to speak on behalf of the Government. . . . I can assure you there is wide-spread resentment in the party at your activities, and a period of silence on your part would be welcome.'[2]

It is clear, then, that in both major parties, external pressures, with the one exception of pressure from the organized body of

[1] McKenzie, p. 422.
[2] Quoted by Kingsley Martin, *Harold Laski*. London, 1953, p. 182.

constituency workers, are unimportant compared to internal pressures. A Member obviously cannot rid himself of attitudes, friendships and obligations which he acquired before entering Parliament. His judgement may be tipped in one direction or another by a chance conversation with a non-political friend whom he has known since childhood, whose common sense he admires, and whose respect he does not want to lose. But, generally speaking, his attitude is determined by what he hears publicly and privately in the House. In the great majority of cases he does not feel the need to think at all, if the matter is unimportant to his constituents or uninteresting to him personally. He gladly follows the lead given by the leaders of his parliamentary party, whether in or out of office, because he shares their general outlook and trusts them not to depart from it in the details of policy for which they are responsible. If atomic energy or coalmining, about which I know nothing, are under discussion, it would not occur to me to take a stand against the party line. It is only when a topic arises of overwhelming importance to the country, or of which the Member can claim to have made a special study, or which closely affects his constituency, that he begins to consider his duty as a Member of Parliament in addition to his duty as a member of his party. That is the explanation of sheep-like voting in the party's lobby. I do not find it shocking. It would be no more impressive, and certainly less conducive to strong and steady government, if every Member on every occasion found it necessary to refer to his conscience every item of advice he was given by his party's acknowledged expert on the subject, since on 95 per cent of such subjects, his conscience would have nothing to say to him at all. We are here only concerned with the other 5 per cent.

Let us first consider the instances where party discipline is deliberately lifted by allowing a free vote of the House and exposing the Member to the full play of external pressures.

There are more free votes than is often realized. During the last six years the totals have been: 1952, thirteen; 1953, thirteen; 1954, eight; 1955, nine; 1956, thirty-one (many of them connected with the Death Penalty Abolition Bill); 1957, fourteen.[1]

---

[1] Figures supplied by the Research Department of the House of Commons Library.

Several of these were votes on Private Bills promoted by local authorities. Though the principle of allowing an untrammelled expression of opinion on such occasions is a sound one, the practice is often absurd. Say the Rochester Corporation Bill is under discussion. In theory, Members crowd the Chamber to listen to the arguments for and against the Bill, and are led to their decision in much the same way as a jury in a murder trial. In fact, only a small proportion of those who will ultimately decide the fate of Rochester listen to the arguments at all. They are busy elsewhere. The division bells ring, and Members arrive from all quarters of the House expecting to find a Whip standing at the entrance to the appropriate lobby. There is no Whip; it is a free vote. Aghast, the Member tries to discover from his nearest neighbours whether Rochester should be allowed its Bill or not, while the Town Clerk of Rochester gnaws his finger-nails in his seat under the gallery. It may be so slight a consideration as that the Member himself represents a county-borough like Rochester which will decide him in its favour; or a chance reminder that the Bill includes a clause to permit municipal trading which may decide him against it. It is fair to add that such Bills usually receive their Second Reading, and are passed for more serious examination to a Committee; but the absurdity of the process illustrates the advantages of whipped voting. It is impossible for Members to keep abreast of all matters which come before Parliament and form a balanced opinion on each of them.

That is an exceptional case. Usually free votes are awarded on occasions when considerable public interest has already been aroused, and national organizations have been stimulated to a frenzy of lobbying by the knowledge that no Member can shelter behind the dictation of his party. Often the cry is raised outside that a proposal should be decided by a free vote, simply because Government policy is known to be luke-warm or hostile. This is the almost annual practice of the National Federation of Old Age Pensioners, who naturally hope that enough Members will surrender to constituency pressure if a free vote is allowed. The same person will often insist that a matter should be 'taken out of party politics', and simultaneously promise to vote for any party which includes it in its election programme, without noticing the contradiction. Or the Opposition, in order to embarrass the Government, may call for a free vote on an issue which unites their own side and splits their opponents. These tactics rarely succeed, for the House has come to agree, within narrow limits, on the occasions when a free vote is justified. It cannot be on a topic which involves a large segment of Government policy, or heavy expenditure. It cannot be used simply as an excuse to save the Cabinet from coming to a decision. The issue must be one which arouses strong moral or religious feelings, and where genuine doubt is already known to exist in the House or in the country. Thus the subjects for free votes choose themselves: horror-comics; Kosher killing; Sunday Observance; staghunting; revision of the prayer-book. In other words, subjects on which there are known to be strong differences of opinion on both sides of the House, where a Government's prestige and general policy will not be affected whichever way the vote goes, and where majority opinion in the country is not clear but constituencies are deeply interested.

Members of Parliament are less fond of free votes than is supposed. They know that whichever way they use their unaccustomed freedom, they are likely to offend half of their constituents. It may be a subject on which the Member holds no strong views of his own; but if it is one on which he holds opposite views to those of a majority of his local supporters, he is bound to ask himself whether the removal of the whip at Westminster means that it can immediately be reimposed by the party in his constituency. Is he obliged to do his best to discover the majority view of his electors, and speak and vote in accordance with it, whether he agrees with it or not? If so, should he be guided by the views of those who voted for him and threaten not to vote for him again if he ignores their wishes, more than by the views of his electorate as a whole? Is he speaking for himself, in the expectation that other speakers in the debate will reflect the views of a majority of his constituents when he does not share them, just as he will be speaking on behalf of unknown millions in the country who agree with him? And if, during the course of the debate, a spokesman from the front bench expresses strongly the Government's own view of the matter, to what extent is that a

3*

limitation on a back-bench Member's complete freedom to disagree with it? These questions will be further considered in the next chapter, in the context of the controversy on capital punishment, which produced the most notorious free votes of recent times. In theory the answer to them all was given by Mr R. A. Butler in the debate on the Festival of Britain (Sunday opening) Bill, when he said, 'I trust that all votes will be given according to the prickings of conscience, and not under pressure of post-cards'.[1] But it is not so simple.

Free votes are exercises in the relationship between a Member and his constituents: all other votes involve his relationship with his party in Parliament, and particularly with his Whips and party leaders. On the rare occasions when a Member feels impelled to oppose his party, to what extent is pressure put on him to refrain from doing so, what penalties are invoked if he refuses, and by what methods is trouble of this sort settled behind the scenes?

Pressure is exerted in two directions, by back-bench Members on party-leaders, and by Whips on back-benchers. It would be wrong to think of them in a state of permanent combat, yet almost no week passes in his parliamentary life when a Member of the Government party does not try to persuade a Minister to do something which the Minister does not wish to do, or when the Member is not himself under some degree of suspicion in the Whips' office. Those who accuse Members of Parliament of sheepish inactivity would be surprised to discover with what energy most of them struggle in the pen. What other purpose have they in being there at all, except to use their influence on behalf of their constituents or their own ideas? There is no sense in repeating that Members are shackled by their Whips, when the newspapers carry an almost daily story of some 'revolt'—back-bench Conservative pressure on the Minister of Housing to amend the Rent Act, or on the Chancellor of the Exchequer to exclude retrospective legislation from the Finance Bill; Socialist dissatisfaction with the party's policy on nuclear weapons, or murmurs of protest against its new proposals to control private industry. Few of these reports are baseless, and their frequency is

[1] *Hansard*, vol. 481, col. 542. November 23rd, 1950.

a measure of the amount of flexibility left within the parliamentary parties.

There is no barrier between front and back benches, except that imposed by shyness, inexperience, or diffidence in troubling an important and busy man. Most back-bench Members have served on terms of equality with their leading spokesmen before their promotion, or have themselves been Ministers in the past. Friendship is not killed by disagreement, nor by the conferment of distinction on one man and not on another. A Minister does not easily forget the temptations to dissent and the pangs of doubt to which he, too, was subject on the back benches. They are all Members of Parliament. Disagreement is a staple part of their existence. 'Loyalty' is a word heard far less at Westminster than outside, because it is a quality open to such different interpretations and reservations, that it ceases to have much meaning. Is a back-bench Member disloyal to his Minister if he tells him privately that he thinks the Minister has made an error of judgement? Or only if he says so in public? In both cases, the Minister's job is made no easier, but it would not occur to him to resent it. All he would ask is that such disagreement should first be expressed privately, to give him a chance to explain the motives and implications of his policy which cannot be publicly stated, and to modify it, perhaps, to meet the Member's point-of-view before their disagreement leads to an open row.

 The Whips' function is not to stifle genuine dissent, but to canalize it as far as possible along channels hidden from the public gaze. The notion that a Whip stands over a rebellious Member, expostulating against his disloyalty and threatening him with the loss of all chance of future office, is remote from the truth. Apart from their thankless duty as janitors to save the Government from chance defeat in the division lobbies, they must act as a two-way Intelligence service, to warn Ministers of trouble stirring on the back benches, and to warn Members of the consequences of carrying disagreement to extreme lengths. 'It is persuasion rather than bullying that is the rule,' Mr Herbert Morrison has written; 'it is reasoning with a recalcitrant Member rather than coercion.'[1] Bullying would do no good, because the Member has the final

[1] Herbert Morrison, *Government and Parliament*. Oxford, 1954, p. 104.

word. A threat to his political prospects would make no sense, with a front-bench of Ministers daily on view, each one of whom has at some period of his career flouted the Whips on a major issue. 'If you must, you must,' is their method of approach to a potential rebel. 'But I beg you to think it over. See the Minister first. Think of his difficulties, and the boost you will be giving to the Opposition. And at least don't vote against the Government. Surely it would be enough for you merely to abstain?'

Nobody who has had experience of one of these interviews can have come away with a feeling of outrage or disgust. One's indignation is often the less afterwards than before. So subtle is their relationship, that a Member will, for instance, deliberately warn his Whip that he intends to move an amendment against the Government on a Standing Committee, and add, 'Do you think you can get enough of our people together to defeat it?' To an outsider it must seem as incomprehensible that a Member should thus help to organize the rejection of his own motion as that a painter should canvass the Hanging Committee of the Royal Academy to reject his picture. But the Member knows very well that his warning has created confidence in the Whip's mind that he is not the sort of man to gain his object by trickiness. If his motion has any validity, it will be more likely to find acceptance with the Government or its purpose met in another way, than if he had tried to carry his point by storm and surprise. If it has not, he has at least been able to put his argument and drive it to its conclusion in a vote.

Trust and mutual respect are the motive power of this curious back-stage mechanism of politics. Trust that a Member will not defy his party on a sudden whim, or for purposes of self-advertisement; trust that the Whips will not blight his reputation or deny him the few privileges in their gift because of an isolated act of insubordination; trust that the Minister will give due weight to a serious objection moderately presented, even when it causes him embarrassment. This attitude extends outside the Whips' office to the whole of Parliament. The standing of a Member with the Opposition as well as with his own party depends largely on his method of dissent. To curry favour with his opponents by attacking his own side is as contemptible as to conceal his profoundest disagreement in the hope of gaining favour with the Whips. There are turns of phrase in parliamentary speaking which carry the same sort of double meaning as the language of diplomacy. A Labour Member will say to a Minister of the present Government: 'It is utterly disagraceful that the Minister should treat these poor people so callously.' A Conservative would say: 'While I am glad that my Right Honourable Friend has been able to do so much for them, I would like to suggest for his consideration two further steps which his Ministry might take.' Both speakers mean exactly the same thing, one much less, the other much more, than he actually says. Hypocrisy? I do not think it can be described as such, when the whole House recognizes the nuances of the words used. If the Conservative had spoken like the Socialist, there would have been a hoot of approval from the Opposition, but a hoot of derision too.

Apart from normal politeness to his leaders in public, an essential precaution of the intending dissenter is to declare his disagreement beforehand in the privacy of a party committee. Each party has a committee which concerns itself with the work of each of the major departments of State, and a general committee open to the whole parliamentary party, known in the Conservative Party as the 1922 Committee, and in the Labour Party as the Party Meeting. The appropriate Minister is sometimes present at his own party's committees, and a Whip is assigned to attend each of them on every occasion. No more than formal minutes are made, proceedings are confidential, and in Conservative committees no vote is ever taken: the general opinion of the committee is assessed by the tone of the speeches and the murmurs of approval or disapproval which they arouse. Some of the best debating in Parliament is heard on these informal occasions: a Member who finds it difficult to state his views on the floor of the House in under twenty minutes, on a committee will make the same argument more effectively in three.

Party committees have a threefold purpose: to give Members background information which they may find useful for forthcoming debates or for their constituency speeches; to give Ministers and Whips an indication of the strength of feeling on an issue, and the degree of opposition within their own party which they will have to face publicly if they fail to bury it privately; and to give cohesion to the party as a whole. It will be obvious that the system depends upon maximum privacy. Recent leakages to the press have made it difficult for Ministers to say anything to party committees which could not as well be said in public, and in addition to the unpleasantness of suspicion attaching to every person who has been present at a meeting from which such a leak has occurred, Members themselves feel an inhibition from saying what they think.

Even in normal conditions, however, a Minister cannot state in detail the proposals of the Government before he has stated them to the House. One notable exception to the rule, recorded by Mr Morrison, was when the Labour Government gave advance notice to the Parliamentary Labour Party of their intention to introduce peace-time conscription, 'since it was not in the party programme and was likely to come as a shock.' But a Minister will normally give the committee no more than an idea of the considerations which are in his mind as he approaches a decision and of the alternatives open to him, and then sit back to listen to the ideas of his back-benchers. For example, the Minister of Agriculture might state to the Agricultural Committee the arguments for and against the deliberate spreading of myxamatosis; or the Leader of the House might open in general terms at the 1922 Committee a discussion on Members' pay. It is difficult to imagine that either of them would deliberately flout the majority feeling of the committee; and if they did so, those who had spoken strongly would feel that they had given all the advance notice required by convention before expressing their dissent in public.

On the other hand, it would be rare for a Committee to force a Minister to reverse a major aspect of policy previously declared. At the most, policy might be changed in response to back-bench pressure, by crab-like movements tending in the same general direction but slipping gently sideways to meet the criticisms expressed. An example is the amendment to the Landlord and Tenant Act in the spring of 1958, to mitigate the hardships caused by the Rent Act. It was public knowledge that a group of Conservative back-bench Members had confronted the Minister of Housing with examples of hardship in their own constituencies, and his own information had led him to anticipate the trouble. By agreement the change was made in a manner least likely to tamper with the main purpose of the Rent Act or to damage the Government's prestige.

The criticism has been made that the committee system prevents the public from knowing the genuine opinions of their representatives, and that a measure would often be defeated in the House if Members continued to act in accordance with the views they expressed in private. 'The sheep escape from the fold,' wrote Sir Ivor Jennings, with typical contempt for the back-bench Member, 'and assemble in flocks of their own choosing, but they can always be called back by the division bell.'[1] There are three answers to that: first, many back-bench criticisms are anticipated by Ministers from views previously expressed in committee ('the party wouldn't stand for it'); secondly, draft Bills or administrative proposals are often altered as a result of what the Minister hears in private before they even reach the public eye; and thirdly, everyday experience shows that when pushed too far, a recalcitrant Member will have no hesitation in carrying his dissent to the open Chamber. But it is true that in committee Members fly kites which they would not fly in public. They feel less reticence in expressing points of view based on rumour or chance examples. And in moments of crisis for the party they will temper their public criticism, unless impelled by a strength of feeling which cannot be concealed. The committee system does not so much whittle down dissent, as divert it at a preliminary stage into channels where it is all the more effective for being private.

The foregoing applies in general to both major parties. But there is one significant difference between them. On all important matters, the Labour Party insist upon the agreement of their Members to the party's majority decisions: the Conservative Party leaves compliance or dissent to the discretion of the individual Member. A Labour Member who votes against his party has committed a breach of its Standing Orders, to which there is no Conservative equivalent. Every Labour candidate is required to pledge obedience to these Standing Orders. They are quite specific: 'The privilege of membership of the Parliamentary

[1] Sir Ivor Jennings, *Parliament*. Cambridge, 1957, p. 380.

Labour Party involves the acceptance of the decision of the Party Meeting,' they begin; and then follows the famous conscience clause: 'The Party recognizes the right of individual Members to abstain from voting on matters of deeply held personal con- scientious conviction.' Mr Attlee justified this apparently in- tolerant rule in this way: 'It is only a recognition of the duty of a Member to represent his constituents. A Labour candidate stands for certain definite principles, and is supported by men and women who have chosen him to represent them and to carry out these principles. They have therefore the right to expect that he will faithfully carry them out. The pledge is only an honest and explicit avowal of the discipline which is necessary for all effective work in Parliament by a political party.'[1]

So broad a generalization seems to beg several major questions. For instance, if such a pledge is necessary, how have the Con- servative Party managed without it to avoid internal dissensions more successfully than their opponents? Again, while the whole Labour Party may be agreed on their principles, one Member may take quite a different view from another on the particular methods by which they should be implemented. And if the main purpose of the Standing Orders is to ensure that a Member truly represents his constituents, what is to happen when his consti- tuents and the Parliamentary Party disagree?

These questions are not academic. The failure to answer them has been one of the main sources of weakness to the Labour Party. To say that the problem does not exist, when it so evidently does, is simply to magnify it. 'We get into a Party meeting upstairs,' Mr Bevan has said from painful personal experience. 'Then we come down to the floor of the House of Commons. We make speeches, and if they do not accord with what has just been decided in private upstairs, we are threatened with expulsion. Is that democracy? It is conspiracy. . . . The caucus is getting more powerful than the electorate itself.'[2] Sometimes dissident Socialists swallow their pride and their convictions, and refrain from making the speeches which they long to make. Sometimes they make them, and withdraw them later. Very rarely, as during the

[1] C. R. Attlee, *The Labour Party in Perspective*. London, 1949, p. 87.
[2] *Manchester Guardian*, February 4th, 1956.

passage of the Conscription Bill in 1947, have the rebels succeeded, without penalty, in gaining their point in the House,
having lost it in committee. But the recent history of the party
shows that in many cases, disagreement by individual Labour
Members, or groups of them, has been followed by the withdrawal of the whip and expulsion. In the later stages of the
1945–50 Parliament it was the National Executive which initiated
action against certain Labour Members on policy grounds: they
all stood as Independents at the election of 1950, and all were
defeated. In March 1955, it was the Party Meeting which took the
first step, and withdrew the whip from Mr Bevan by 141 votes to
122: he was only saved by a single vote from expulsion from the
party by the National Executive. These and other instances are
all well remembered and recorded: the details need not be
repeated here.[1]

The present conscience clause, redrafted in 1952 when Standing Orders were reintroduced, differs from its predecessor in
failing to specify the type of circumstances in which a Labour
Member is justified in openly disagreeing with his party. The 1946
version read: 'It is recognized that on certain matters, for example
religion and temperance, Members may have good grounds for
conscientious scruples, and in such cases they may refrain from
voting.' The greater ambiguity of the present version, which
simply refers to 'matters of deeply held personal conscientious
conviction', leaves it in doubt whether it only covers subjects
which would normally be left to a free vote of the House, or
includes major issues of foreign and domestic policy, such as the
hydrogen bomb, on which deeply conscientious convictions can
certainly be held.

When the Victory for Socialism group, in defiance of official
party policy, attempted in February 1958 to arouse a nation-wide
protest against Britain's reliance on the nuclear deterrent, they
claimed that their purpose was to 'recreate agitation for the
application of fundamental Socialist principles.' One of their
parliamentary spokesmen, Mr Zilliacus, added that the issue of the

[1] For a summary of the Conscription Bill, Nenni telegram, Ireland Bill, and other
instances in the period of the post-war Labour Government, see J. M. Burns, 'The
Parliamentary Labour Party in Great Britain'. *The American Political Science Review*,
XLIV. December, 1950.

hydrogen bomb was 'a matter of conscience and principle, and not one of obeying party discipline or majority decisions'.[1] Thus, by two different approaches, they were claiming consistency between their attitude and party Standing Orders. They were applying Socialist principles, and so could not be guilty of thwarting the main purpose of the party in Parliament; and they were disagreeing with the party on legitimate grounds of conscience. The crisis was overcome by side-tracking the main issue. The rebels accepted the National Executive's ban on forming a party within the party to gain support for their ideas. But this still left the main question unanswered: is a Labour Member free to say publicly what he thinks on a major matter of Socialist policy, which certainly involves his deepest moral scruples?

When the same question arises in the Conservative Party, as it arose at the time of the Suez crisis, the answer has always been unquestionably, Yes. Conservatives in Parliament do not demand agreement with party decisions. They do not expel their Members or withdraw the whip for disobedience. The whip has only once been withdrawn in the last forty years. It is far more frequently refused *by* the Member than *to* him. How then could Mr Morrison write: 'The technique of the two great parties in handling disciplinary problems is much the same, though the Labour Party is more formally democratic,'[2] or Mr Attlee, that 'the Conservative Member who votes against his party may be dealt with even more drastically than the Labour Member'?[3] The comparative rarity of major Conservative quarrels is not due to greater docility among Conservatives. It will be remembered how Winston Churchill led his supporters night after night into the Opposition lobby during the passage of the India Bill. Nor is it due to an exaggerated sense of party loyalty. Conservatives can be utterly ruthless in intriguing against their leaders, when they consider their policies to be a danger to the country.

They have come to accept that such incidents as Munich, as Suez, will from time to time arise, that deep and passionate disagreements will flare up between colleagues, and that instead

[1] *The Times.* March 1st, 1958.
[2] *Government and Parliament*, p. 129.
[3] *The Labour Party in Perspective*, p. 87.

of dealing with them by means of expulsion, ostracism or written codes of conduct, the party should allow each Member to do as he thinks right, and let subsequent events show whether he was justified. 'Look at the careers of any of the last three leaders of the Conservative Party, or, for that matter, of the last three Chairmen,' said Lord Hailsham in April 1958. 'None of them, I venture to assert, has always been exactly orthodox in all their doings. None of us, at one time or another, has scrupled to criticize party policy or party tactics. You may be absolutely sure in joining us that you will be encouraged to show the same independence of mind and objectivity of outlook that we have claimed for ourselves.'[1]

That is true of the party in Parliament. It is not yet as true as it should be of the party outside.

[1] Speech at Caxton Hall, London. April 22nd, 1958.

Chapter Four

CAPITAL PUNISHMENT

Fluctuations in opinion on death sentence—summary of controversy 1929–1957 —was it a party issue?—the Conservative abolitionists—summary of arguments on both sides—fear of increase in murders—religious significance of hanging—attempted murder—division of public opinion—anti-abolitionist views of Conservative party conference—constituency pressure—constituency criticisms of myself—confusion in Parliament about Member's duty—Lord Salisbury's definition of it—were the public consulted?—should capital punishment have been an election issue?—Members' attitude to changing public opinion—Conservative abolitionists modify their attitude—their reasons for compromising

THE CONTROVERSY over the death penalty raised, in a particularly vivid form, the problem of the free vote. The Suez crisis, discussed in the next chapter, raised an acute problem of party loyalty. Both together illustrate nearly all the disputed aspects of the relationship between a Member, his constituents and his party. In the sixth chapter of this book, I shall examine the problem of dissent within a still narrower frame-work, the events of the past two years in a single constituency, my own.

The partially successful attempt in 1955–56 to abolish the death sentence for murder was the penultimate stage in a controversy which has extended over one hundred and fifty years. There is no subject on which men's minds have been liable to more violent fluctuations. Boswell could take Sir Joshua Reynolds from Newgate to Tyburn in the same coach as the man about to be hanged, and regard it as no more than an interesting excursion. Today we find such behaviour incomprehensible, but are unable to make the mental leap ahead to the middle of the next century, and look back on our own time with the eyes of our descendants. Surely they will regard it as very strange that a nation which had led the world in penal reform, should have lagged so far behind it in abolishing the most terrible punishment of all? We pride ourselves on having proceeded cautiously but consistently. But British opinion on the death sentence has moved by fits and starts. Support for abolition was almost as strong in the second half of the nineteenth century as it is today, and in 1948 Winston Churchill could even claim that it was a notion outdated by events: 'Those,' he wrote, 'who in a human age which has multiplied executions in cold blood to an extent that would be amazing to former generations, stand against the storm and hold up *their mild Victorian lamp* in the blackness of the twentieth century.'[1] (My italics.) It was just because the world had passed through a period of unprecedented carnage that the modern reformers felt that it was necessary 'to dissociate ourselves once and for all from the tendencies that degraded the dignity of human beings, and to proclaim to the world our rejection of the doctrine that the State has the right to take human life in time of peace.'[2] Between those who took that view, and those who declared it to be nauseating sentimentality, there was a great gulf. Abolitionists thought that the death-sentence was itself an evil: retentionists (I use the jargon of 1956) that it was no more indefensible than imprisonment, a punishment to fit the crime. All the statistical evidence that was amassed failed to bridge the gulf. Neither side convinced the other, and both claimed to have the angels with them.

The parliamentary battle was prolonged and complex, though the question put to Parliament at each stage was clear enough: shall hanging be retained or abolished as a punishment for murder? Before discussing the effect of public opinion on Parliament, and *vice versa*, it might clarify the story to recall its main phases.

In 1929 a Resolution in the House of Commons proposed the abolition of capital punishment. There was no vote on the main question, but the debate led to the appointment of a Select Committee, composed of seven Labour Members, six Conservatives and two Liberals. A majority of the Committee reported in 1930 in favour of abolition for an experimental period of five years, but the six Conservatives objected, and withdrew from the Committee two weeks before its report was published. Nothing more was done till 1938, when a motion was carried in the House of Commons to give effect to the majority report, but the Government refused to act, and in the next year an Amendment to the

---

[1] Quoted by Sir Ernest Gowers, *A Life for a Life?* London, 1956, p. 60.
[2] Lord Templewood, *The Shadow of the Gallows*. London, 1951, p. 12.

Criminal Justice Bill on the same lines was defeated. After the war, in 1948, the same Amendment, proposing the suspension of the death penalty for five years, was passed in the Commons on a free vote by 245 to 222, against the advice of Mr Chuter Ede, then Home Secretary. The Clause was rejected by the Lords by 181 to 28. As a way of escaping an imminent quarrel between Lords and Commons, the Government set up a Royal Commission in 1949, under the chairmanship of Sir Ernest Gowers, to examine the whole question of capital punishment. The Commission was prohibited by its terms of reference from stating its view whether the death sentence should be abolished or not, but the evidence gathered in this and foreign countries was of great value in subsequent debates, and the Chairman of the Commission later wrote a book declaring that he had personally been converted to the abolitionist cause.[1] Just before the publication of the Royal Commission's report, in 1953, Mr Silverman introduced his Death Penalty Suspension Bill: it was rejected in the Commons by 256 to 195, mainly on the grounds that, as the report had not yet been published, the Bill was premature. In February 1955, three months before the General Election, in the Commons debate on the Royal Commission's report, an amendment advocating the suspension of the death penalty for five years, was again lost, by 245 to 214. A year later, in a general debate in the new House of Commons, abolition won the day, on a free vote but against Government advice, by 293 to 262, and in March 1956 Mr Silverman introduced his Death Penalty Abolition Bill, which was carried on Second Reading by 286 to 262. The Lords rejected it in July by 238 to 95. The same situation had arisen as in 1948. To solve it, the Home Secretary, Major Lloyd-George, brought in a Government compromise Bill, limiting the death penalty to the more terrible forms of murder, and this became law in March 1957.

Thus, in the space of twenty-six years, the Commons had four times approved the principle of abolition, and three times rejected it. The Lords had twice rejected the advice of the Commons, and two full-scale inquiries had been undertaken into the ramifications of the problem. The emotions aroused by these events were lasting and intense.

[1] Sir Ernest Gowers, *A Life for a Life?* London, 1956.

Was it a party issue? In theory, not. But throughout, dating from the resignation of all the Conservative members from the Select Committee in 1930, Socialists tended to support abolition, and Conservatives to oppose it, and the broad division on party lines in Parliament was reproduced more rigidly among party-workers in the country. It would be too much of a coincidence to suppose that 97 per cent of Labour Members would wish to abolish capital punishment, and 87 per cent of Conservatives would wish to retain it, unless the pressure of party opinion had some influence on their judgement. But it should be remembered that in 1948, when the Labour Party was in power with a large majority, an abolitionist amendment was carried against the advice of the Government; and that when the Conservatives were in office, back-bench Conservative support for abolition continued to increase in spite of the strong warnings of successive Home Secretaries, particularly after the 1955 election, when seventeen of the newly elected Members joined the abolitionists to bring the Conservative abolitionist vote to 47.

In the country, the campaign for abolition was associated with the Socialists, and fervent Conservatives were more inclined to oppose it from the start for that reason. The National Campaign for the Abolition of Capital Punishment, which held meetings up and down the country, was organized by such well-known left-wing or pacifist figures as Victor Gollancz, Canon Collins, Arthur Koestler and Reginald Paget. The main burden of the parliamentary battle fell on Sydney Silverman, who was not popular among Conservatives in the country because of his far-left sympathies in other matters, and even Mr Butler's tribute to him as a *justum et tenacem propositi virum*[1] did not remove the Conservative suspicion that he was actuated more by party than moral motives. It was a 'Socialist Bill', and Conservative Members who supported it were 'falling for a Socialist trick to embarrass the Government'. A correspondent to the *Daily Telegraph* wrote: 'The nauseating drivel written by these MPs is enough to raise the gore, and distend the stomach of an ox.'

More important in deciding the Conservative attitude even than suspicion of Labour motives, was the consistency with which

[1] *Hansard*, vol. 564, col. 455. February 6th, 1957.

the Government, supported by the police, prison officers and nearly all the judges, stated their view against abolition. In the opinion of Parliament these warnings must be given full weight, but they limited in no way the right of a Member to vote as he felt right; in the opinion of Conservatives outside Parliament, an abolitionist vote was a defiance not only of the Government's advice, but even of their instructions. To this day many people look on the Conservative abolitionists as rebels; and the fact that many members of the Government itself (including Selwyn Lloyd, Ian Macleod, Derick Heathcoat Amory, Derek Walker-Smith, and even Major Lloyd-George himself, before he became Home Secretary) were recorded as holding abolitionist views, was either unknown or ignored. Nor is the impression that Conservative supporters of Mr Silverman were tainted with left-wing deviationism borne out by an examination of the division lists. Even in 1955 they included such Suez-Group leaders as Lord Hinchingbrooke, Julian Amery and Angus Maude, while Sir Robert Boothby was found in the retentionist lobby. In February 1956, it was even more evident that a 'liberal' outlook in home and foreign affairs had little to do with a Member's attitude to capital punishment: such Conservative Members as John Biggs-Davison, Sir Henry d'Avigdor-Goldsmid, Mrs Emmet, Ted Leather, Richard Pilkington, Brigadier Prior-Palmer, John Rodgers, John Peyton, William Teeling, and, again, Lord Hinchingbrooke and Julian Amery, none of whom could be accused of a tendency to flirt with the Opposition, walked boldly into the Silverman lobby, while all the Ministers mentioned above, except the Home Secretary, were either absent or abstained.

The arguments which were put forward against and in favour of the abolition of capital punishment varied little over the years, and even the report of the Royal Commission only reinforced the evidence already published by the Select Committee twenty years earlier. In brief, the arguments in favour of abolition were: that the death sentence was not a unique deterrent to intending murderers, because the experience of foreign countries where the experiment of abolition had been tried was that the murder-rate was unaffected by it; that execution removes any possibility of redeeming the criminal, or of correcting a mistake in the verdict;

and that the executing of murderers is almost as obscene as the crime of murder itself, leading to sensationalism and the degradation of public standards. The arguments of the retentionists were: that the experience of foreign countries was no guide to the probable effect of abolition in our own, because of differences in national temperament and conditions; that the public, the police and prison warders would be in greater danger of their lives, since criminals would know that murder would only add to their prison sentence, and not result in the loss of their own lives; that, in any case, murder must be set aside from all other crimes by a punishment more severe than any other punishment; and that public opinion was not in favour of abolition.

For the purpose of illustrating the impact of Parliamentary debates on public opinion, I wish to examine only two aspects of the retentionist argument: the fear of an increase in the murder-rate; and the distinction between murder and all other crimes. Fear was undoubtedly a dominant motive; not only fear for a person's own safety and his family's, but fear for the old and solitary. 'Women fear the knock at the door after it is dark,' said Lord Simon in the 1948 debate, thus putting fear into the minds of women who might otherwise never have given a thought to the matter. Eight years later Lord Salisbury told the House of Lords of the letters he had received, 'not from the rich and great, who are cushioned by wealth and position from fear of attack, but from humble folk, and particularly elderly folk, who have often only a frail latch between themselves and violence.'[1] Reading those words next morning, what old and lonely woman did not glance nervously at her door? The point was well rubbed in by Lord Goddard, the Lord Chief Justice:

There was a dreadful case a few weeks ago of a little spinster, four feet nine inches in height, living on the edge of some mining village, and so afraid of being attacked that she had all the windows of her cottage screwed up. A young brute of about 23 broke into that house. He battered that poor little creature to death; all her ribs were broken, and he cut her throat. All he got out of it was a small quantity of rather trivial jewellery. Are those people to be kept alive?[2]

[1] *Hansard*, House of Lords, vol. 198, col. 822. July 10th, 1956.
[2] Col. 742.

These harrowing illustrations, legitimate, perhaps, in a speech by the counsel for the prosecution in a murder trial, diverted public attention from the only proper question: Would the little spinster be in any greater danger if capital punishment were abolished than if it were retained? The Lord Chief Justice was in no doubt that she would, but his last sentence shows that he had an additional motive for executing murderers, the satisfaction of eliminating them as an act of social hygiene. Few other speakers went so far. But cumulatively the effect was exactly the same as that of the notorious advice given by an earlier Chief Justice, Lord Ellenborough, during the debate in 1810 on Sir Samuel Romilly's Bill to abolish capital punishment for the theft of five shillings or over from a shop: 'Repeal this law, and no man can trust himself for an hour out of doors without the most alarming apprehensions that, on his return, every vestige of his property will be swept off by the hardened robber.' Tell the people these things, arouse their fears, dazzle them with the authority of Cabinet Ministers, Judges, the Home Office, police officials and the like, and the people will not only believe them, but will attribute to anyone who points out the reasons why their fears are probably baseless, the character of the murderer himself. The abolition Bill became known as the Murderers' Charter.

I had the reaction in my own postbag two days later: 'I appeal to you to ask the question in Parliament, in view of the no hanging of murderers, will the Government contribute to the cost of pistols for householders, so they can have a useful weapon handy in case of emergency?' From another constituent: 'The fruit of the abolition is already seen in the murder of the day before yesterday.' (No form of abolition had yet taken place.) From a third: 'Surely hanging is at least a small deterrent to murderers?' Yes, of course. But by that time, the impression had been given that hanging was the only punishment capable of deterring a murderer, and that the country was full of evil men waiting for the opportunity to strike which abolition would give them. If the dangers of bad driving were emphasized with equal ferocity, nobody would dare emerge into the street, and the case for punishing dangerous drivers by penal servitude for life would be overwhelming. I do not see how the public could have reacted otherwise. I only wish that the case for retention could have been presented to them in less melodramatic terms.

Then there was the distinction made between murder and all other crimes, which suggested to the public that whether the murder-rate rose or fell after abolition, it would be wrong to remove the 'quasi-religious sense of awe' which, according to the Bishop of Winchester in 1948, an execution arouses in the breasts of all normal men. A really brutal murder is of course an ultimate crime, and deserves an ultimate punishment. But all murders are not brutal (a suicide pact, for instance, or a mercy-killing), and the ultimate punishment is not necessarily death. It is only because we are so accustomed to the execution of a Haigh, that we have come to expect the execution of men like him, and would feel that some injustice had been done if they were kept in prison for life. Robbery with violence and sexual assault on young children have not been punishable by death for a century, and there is no demand that they should be. But if the death-penalty for these crimes had not been abolished, and it were now proposed that it should be, exactly the same emotions would be aroused. We would say that the worst examples of these crimes were at least on a level with the less terrible forms of murder in terms of wickedness, as they often are, and that it would be quite wrong to put criminals of this sort in a category of lesser guilt. That we do not say so is due to habit, and not to reason.

Even stranger is our attitude to attempted murder. Let us imagine two similar cases, of two women who shoot their lovers. In each case the motive is the same, jealousy; the intention is the same, to kill; the weapon is the same, a revolver; and both women are of sound mind. The only difference in the two crimes is that the first woman succeeds in her attempt. The other fails; her lover falls gravely wounded, but does not die. One will be convicted of murder, and, like Ruth Ellis, will be hanged. The second will be convicted of shooting with intent to murder, and will emerge a free woman after a few years in prison. Now, if murder is to be regarded as a crime quite distinct from any other, surely the immediate intention of the criminal, as he or she presses the trigger, should count for more than a mere accident of aim? If it is right to imprison the second woman instead of hanging her, it is wrong to hang the first. The Bishop of Truro said in the 1948 debate, that ' "Whoso sheddeth man's blood, by man shall his blood be shed", has appealed to man as an approximation of justice.' If that is true, then the murderer who fails in his attempt should be left by the public-executioner half-dead. As this is an absurdity, it is time that Bishops reminded us that an approximation of justice is something which our society does not tolerate in any other instance. With few exceptions, they did not do so.

As the debate swayed to and fro between Lords and Commons, most people in the country came to hold one view or the other, and hold it with great conviction. But in the interval between the debates of 1948 and 1955, there was a perceptible swing of opinion in favour of abolition, and among those who wished to retain it there was a growing recognition that even murder can in some instances be a less terrible crime than in others, and therefore deserving a less terrible sentence. In 1948, when the Nuremberg trials were fresh in everybody's mind and crimes of violence were on the increase, a *Daily Telegraph* poll found only 15 per cent in favour of abolition. In February 1956, the Gallup Poll recorded 35 per cent for abolition, or an experimental period of abolition; 32 per cent for retention; 25 per cent undecided; and 7 per cent for degrees of murder. A month later, on the morning of the Second Reading debate on the Silverman Bill, to the question 'If Parliament did in fact abolish or disapprove of the death penalty, would you approve or disapprove?', 45 per cent answered 'approve', and 41 per cent answered 'disapprove'. A *Daily Mirror* poll produced an even more startling majority for abolition among those who had made up their minds. The figures were not wholly reliable. The Bentley and Ruth Ellis cases had stirred millions of people, but the effect of them might not be lasting, or might suddenly be reversed by a single particularly terrible murder. The general impression was that a majority of the public still considered that total abolition was too risky an experiment, but they were prepared for a change in the law of murder which would limit the imposition of the death penalty to the most heinous murders, and murders involving police officers and prison-warders.

This was unmistakably the opinion of the large majority of

Conservative party-workers, and they expressed it with great force both in writing to their Members, particularly to those who had voted for the Silverman Bill, and by public demonstration. In June 1956, at the Conference of the Conservative Women's National Advisory Committee, attended by some two thousand five hundred delegates, 'when Mrs Emmet, the Member for East Grinstead, sought to argue the case for abolition, she was interrupted by shouts of "Shame!" and "Oh!" and was once booed quite loudly. Finally some delegates started a slow hand-clap.'[1] But they reserved the full violence of their attack for the party's annual Conference at Llandudno in October. Thirty-three resolutions were submitted on capital punishment, more than on any other single subject, and all of them opposed total abolition, even for an experimental period. *The Times* report of the debate indicates the strength of feeling:

Mr Geoffrey Beaman (Crewe) was loudly cheered when he said that much sentimental humbug was talked on that subject. Society must be protected not only from murderers, but also, it appeared, from romantic idealists. 'It is no exaggeration to say that Parliament is grossly out of step with public opinion,' he declared amid a rising wave of applause. 'I am disgusted with the Conservative Members of Parliament who yielded . . . (here the cheering drowned the speaker's words). We can thank God that we have a House of Lords.' The one speaker who opposed the motion could often not be heard above the cat-calls and ironical applause.[2]

The conference eventually passed a resolution to retain the death sentence, but to amend the law of murder to limit its application.

Labour Members of Parliament were in no difficulty. Abolition had become almost a principle of party doctrine, but nothing was heard of any trouble in the constituencies of the few Socialists who opposed it. But many Conservative Members who had voted for the Silverman Bill found themselves under heavy pressure to change their minds. In the frequent party committee-meetings in Parliament the pressure was indirect. After all, it was a free vote, the Whips could not interfere, and several members of the Cabinet were known to support abolition. At most, a hint would be

[1] *The Times.* June 13th, 1956.
[2] *Ibid.* October 13th, 1956.

dropped that the controversy was harming the party in the country, and the view was frequently expressed by back-bench retentionists that it was a pity that the matter had been left over to a free vote when the Government itself held such strong views. The abolitionists were regarded with pity more than dislike. They had manœuvred themselves into a jam; they were allied, on what had now become a major political issue, to one of the party's bitterest critics, Mr Sydney Silverman. In the Commons they had won their point of principle. It had been defeated in the Lords, and now they were confronted in their constituencies with the tactical consequences of their partial victory.

I cannot speak for any other Conservative Members. They all rode the storm in their different ways. In my own constituency, on March 13th, 1956, I invited myself to a meeting of the Executive of my local Association, to remind them fully of the reasons why I had supported abolition. I did not convince them, but the general feeling of the meeting was that they acknowledged my right to speak and vote as I felt, although they disagreed with my views and regretted my action. A leading member of the Executive wrote to me afterwards: 'I do not think you need entertain any fears but that your talk was well received last night; you may not have made any converts to your views, but I am sure that many of your listeners now respect your opinion even if they still disagree with you; and that they know you came to your decision after carefully studying this difficult matter.' Unfortunately this attitude was not to last, even among members of the Executive. When during the course of the winter and spring of 1956, I explained my point of view on capital punishment to several branch meetings in the constituency, I had a very chilly reception. It was not only that my audiences considered that I was exposing humble people to danger by selfishly parading my 'conscience' (how I came to hate that word!), but that they found it incomprehensible that a Member of Parliament should set aside the views of a majority of his local supporters in order to express his own.

It was because of the strength of this feeling that I began my speech on February 16th in the House of Commons with the words: 'In both speaking and voting for abolition, I am very conscious of the fact that a majority of my constituents, were they in the same position as myself, would speak and vote in the opposite sense.'[1] No sentence that I have ever uttered has done me greater harm. It was intended to have precisely the opposite effect to that which it did have. It seemed to me that if I had not made this public admission that most of my constituents disagreed with me, I could justifiably have been accused of a breach of faith, for I might have given the false impression to the House that I had their moral backing. As it was, I made it clear that I was expressing my own opinions, and far from leaving Bournemouth's views unexpressed, I told the House that a majority of Bournemouth people were against abolition. Theirs was the only constituency in the whole country whose attitude was stated to Parliament so plainly.

The flood of letters which followed my speech showed that I had greatly miscalculated the public's reaction. My opening sentence, in their view, was not a mitigation but an aggravation of my obstinacy. One of my correspondents put it very plainly: '1. You were elected to *represent* Bournemouth East. 2. You have stated that you believe the majority of your constituents wish to retain the death penalty. 3. You voted directly contrary to the majority wish of your constituents. Will you please say, therefore, what steps we—your constituents—can take to have our wishes truly represented in Parliament?' Another wrote: 'It is news to me that an MP can please himself how he votes.' A third: 'When the members of your constituency gave their votes to send you to Parliament as their Member, they gave you no mandate to speak for them on such a vital matter as the abolition of the death penalty for murder.' And another: 'I have always understood that when I voted for a candidate, his job was to represent me in the House, but I find you only express your own principles, so what is the object of sending you there?' The evidence was unmistakable. There was complete confusion in the public's mind about the duties of Members on such an issue.

No wonder the public were confused, when the confusion extended to Parliament itself. Consider these two comments by Mr Chuter Ede, one of the most experienced of parliamentarians. The first was made during the 1948 debate on capital punishment

[1] *Hansard,* vol. 548, col. 2608. February 16th, 1956.

when, as Home Secretary, he was arguing the Government's case
for retention:

Mr Beverley Baxter: May I ask the Home Secretary what he would say
in this case? Suppose a Member of Parliament finds himself at variance
with the majority opinion in his constituency, should he then speak and
vote against his own conscience?
Mr Ede: No, he should not. I share the view of Burke, that we are not
delegates; but on the other hand, one of our duties is to ensure in
matters like this that we keep respect for the law alive in the hearts of
people who have to submit to its administration.[1]

Both admirable sentiments, but in this case they were contradictory. Was Mr Baxter to vote for abolition, which he personally
thought was right? Or for retention, which alone would satisfy
his constituents' respect for the law?

Seven years later, Mr Ede, robbed by an intervening election
of his office, and now converted to abolition, was much bolder
and more definite:

I doubt very much whether, at the moment, public opinion is in favour
of this change, but I doubt also whether, at any time during the last
hundred years, a plebiscite would have carried any of the great penal
reforms that have been made. . . . There are occasions when this House
has to say that a certain thing is right, even if the public may not at that
moment be of that opinion.[2]

Clearly, some expression was needed of the present Government's conception of the duty of Members in such cases. It was
supplied by Lord Salisbury in a passage of his speech in the House
of Lords, on the Second Reading of the Silverman Bill. It is so
remarkable an exposition of constitutional doctrine, and it has
attracted so surprisingly little attention, that it deserves quoting
and analysing in full.

Lord Salisbury began by saying, 'A free vote means exactly
what it says—it means a vote given according to the individual
conscience of the individual Member of the House'; and then,
after considering some of the arguments for and against capital
punishment, he continued:

[1] *Hansard,* vol. 449, cols. 1084–5. April 14th, 1948.
[2] *Ibid,* vol. 536, col. 2083. February 10th, 1955.

But in any case, if I may say so in their presence, it is not the Judges, the police, the warders, or any other limited section of the population who, under our Constitution, should finally decide a great question of this kind. We all know that it is the British people who should decide. What is the view of the British people on this particular question. . . ? I fully recognize that there has been a movement of opinion since 1948, but how great a movement I do not know, and I do not believe that anyone does. . . . This question of capital punishment has quite definitely not been put before the electorate at the last or, so far as I know, any other General Election. I know, of course, that there are, on occasions, questions, it may be great questions, which blow up suddenly between elections, and on which the electorate cannot, in the nature of things, be consulted. In such a case it has always been, I believe I am right in saying, the traditional practice of Parliament that Members should use their best judgement in the interests of their constituents and the country.

But, my Lords, I cannot believe that this is one of the cases to which that practice should properly be applied. After all, this question of the abolition of the death penalty is no sudden issue, utterly unforeseen, which could not possibly have been raised at the General Election. It is not a new issue at all. Moreover, it is known to be one about which the British people are at best doubtful. If no Party liked to tackle it— and no Party, either Liberal, Labour or Conservative did put it on their programme—one would have expected at any rate that those Members who are now promoting the Bill as a matter of such urgent importance that it brooks no delay at all, would have made it, so far as they could, an issue at the Election. But I had the curiosity to inquire what mention of capital punishment there had been in the Election addresses of those Members in all parties who have supported this Bill in the House of Commons. What did I find? Not one single one had ever mentioned the subject in his Election address.

I do not say what I have said in any spirit of criticism of those Members concerned. But I want merely to make it clear—and this, I may say, is emphasized in nearly every letter I have received against this Bill—that the British people have never been consulted at all on a matter in which they are deeply and personally concerned. If I am told that consultation at a General Election on an individual issue of this kind is valueless, because the decision at an Election is reached not on a single issue, but on the programme of a party as a whole, I should reply that there was a great deal of truth in that, but that it was equally true with regard to other measures said to have been approved by the electorate in recent history. For instance, in the case of nationalization. . . . That was not so in the case of capital punishment. The

4

electors have had no opportunity of any kind of testifying to their views.

Lord Templewood, in the speech with which he introduced the Bill, enunciated a doctrine which I must confess was new, and slightly shocking to me. It was that where Parliament considers that the British people are not competent to judge, Parliament can quite properly ignore their views—that is to say, to come to a decision without consultation with them. I think he said that, without that, it would have been impossible to make any advance at all in reforms of various kinds. I entirely reject that doctrine. It seems to me quite impossible for Parliament in this country to pay lip-service to democracy in theory and not accept its implications in practice. To say that we trust the people when the people happen to agree with us, and to fail to trust the people in practice, when the people happen to take a rather different view—that way, to my mind, lies the destruction of free democracy.[1]

It should be remembered that Lord Salisbury was advancing this argument as part of his case against abolition. If he had been speaking on the constitutional issue divorced from a highly controversial subject on which he held strong personal views, it is doubtful whether he would have used such categorical language. He was also speaking as a senior member of the Government, which had suffered a defeat in the Commons and was hoping to retrieve it in the Lords. And as Leader of the House of Lords, which at that moment was again under critical scrutiny, he was naturally anxious to repeat the triumph of 1948, when the Lords appeared paradoxically to be the protectors of the people's interests against the obstinate self-righteousness of their elected representatives in the Commons. In spite of these considerations, Lord Salisbury's definition of the relationship between people and Parliament is the most important made in recent years.

The bones of his argument are: This is a great issue. Only the people should decide great issues, unless they arise so suddenly that there is no time to consult them. In this case there was plenty of time, but the advocates of abolition failed in their duty; they did not consult the people. There is good reason to believe that if the people had been consulted, they would have objected strongly. So abolitionist Members are not only ignoring their electors, but defying them. The public must be trusted all the

[1] *Hansard*, House of Lords, vol. 198, cols. 822–6. July 10th, 1956.

time, and we must be guided by their views when they are ascertainable, whether we personally consider them right or wrong. Anything else makes nonsense of our democracy.

But the public *were* consulted. There has scarcely been another subject on which so many people have expressed such strong views so volubly over so long a period. Even discounting the pre-war debates, which the war might have obliterated from the public mind, capital punishment was under constant discussion in Parliament, at meetings outside, in the press, and on the radio and television. Every publication of an opinion-poll, every dramatic murder trial and execution, raised the matter afresh. Silverman's Bill did not creep in slyly and unannounced. It exploded with an impact that could be felt in every corner of the country. Members of Parliament received more letters on capital punishment even than on the Suez crisis, with which the later stages of the controversy were intermingled. They did not know the exact numerical proportion of abolitionists to retentionists in their constituencies, for there was no method of calculating it. But each Member knew with fair accuracy, by combining his instinct for public opinion with the evidence of his correspondence, conversations, public meetings and reports of his agent, how the balance in his constituency lay. That was not his problem; his problem was to decide whether to force himself to agree with it if he did not already do so.

It should have been raised as an issue at the General Election, says Lord Salisbury. If it had been, the verdict of the people on this one subject could not have been disentangled from their verdict on all the other, more important, subjects, such as nationalization, to choose Lord Salisbury's own example. It is quite true that if a candidate had stated his views on capital punishment in his election address, he would probably have had some reaction at his meetings. But the public would then have reacted far less definitely than they did later to the Silverman Bill, when it came before Parliament at a quiet period between elections, and could be considered in isolation from other topics over a longer time, and in a mood less influenced by purely party conflict.

As it happened, however, there was no reason for any group of electors not to know their Member's views on this subject when he appealed for their renewed support at the election of 1955. Less than three months before the dissolution of Parliament on May 6th, the great debate of February 10th had taken place in the House of Commons, on the Royal Commission's report and Silverman's amendment to suspend the death sentence for an experimental period of five years. The division-lists had been fully analysed, and local newspapers, like those in my own constituency, had given great prominence to the way in which their Member had voted. I voted for abolition. My attitude was not criticized at my adoption meeting, and was only referred to three or four times during the course of the election itself. But it was widely known, and I can scarcely imagine a more direct method in which my views could have been placed before the electorate than by the coincidence of the debate in Parliament so shortly followed by the General Election.

If a candidate's attitude to capital punishment is a suitable subject for mention in his election address, should he not also state his views on a whole range of similar subjects, which would probably be occasions for a free vote if they arose during the ensuing Parliament? Stag-hunting, for instance, or homosexuality, or the Jewish method of slaughtering animals. But if this became the practice, two results would follow. The electorate might become so interested in the peculiarities of the candidates' opinions on these minor topics, that they would pay less attention to the real point of the election; while the weaker candidates would be so anxious not to offend their supporters that they would be tempted to commit themselves to attitudes which they might later regret. If, for instance, a candidate had promised his electors not to support any proposal to change the law relating to homosexuals, and subsequently was convinced by the publication of the Wolfenden Report that a change was necessary, what answer would he have for constituents who reproached him with a breach of faith? This strikes me as the basic objection to Lord Salisbury's suggestion. Members of Parliament should not be expected to bind themselves in advance by precise definitions of their points of view on every topic of this sort, because their purpose in going to Westminster is to expose their beliefs and prejudices to argument and new information. The electors can judge by what kind of a man he is, whether their Member is likely to express a sensible considered judgement, and they can bring constant pressure on him. The debate does not cease when the election is over; it is only just beginning. I cannot believe that Lord Salisbury was wholly right. The prolonged discussion of capital punishment in 1956 was a better method of discovering and informing public opinion and of influencing the decisions of Parliament, than if, as he suggested, it had been made an election issue in the previous year.

Naturally, every Member will give great weight to the opinions of his constituents when he makes up his mind on such a complex subject. If in the end he decides that he cannot vote as the majority wish him to vote, it does not mean that he is ignoring their views, but that other considerations, such as the opinions of experts like Sir Ernest Gowers or churchmen like Archbishop Temple, and his own study of the experiences of other countries, have outweighed in his mind the pressure from his constituency. Is this so very wrong? Englishmen are accustomed to deciding controversies by majority, but they are usually anxious that the minority feeling should also be expressed. There were probably few constituencies in the whole country where a plebiscite on the morning of February 16th, 1956, would have produced an absolute majority for abolition. But if every Member had felt bound to speak and vote in the sense of the majority feeling in his own constituency, and for safety's sake, counted the doubtfuls as retentionists, the huge minority support for abolition in the country would scarcely have been expressed in Parliament at all. There were thousands of people in Bournemouth, some of whom had voted for me, and some not, who agreed with my views. I became their spokesman. John Eden, the Member for Bournemouth West, took the opposite view. If I had immediately succumbed to majority pressure, there would have been no local representative of the minority. This difference of opinion between John Eden and myself, I argued in a letter to the local paper, 'simply reflects the divisions of opinion in the Cabinet, the Church, Parliament, and almost any gathering of men and women. Why should Bournemouth pretend to a unanimity on this subject which certainly does not exist here or elsewhere?'

If there had been any indication that opinion was swinging against abolition, as it undoubtedly was in 1948, or that the minority was static, I should have had much more hesitation in voting as I did. The evidence of the public-opinion polls, making every allowance for inaccuracy, showed the opposite. There was a bare majority for retention in the country as a whole, and it was decreasing monthly, in spite of the solemn warnings of the Home Office, the party-political slant given to the controversy, and the quasi-religious arguments by which judgement was dulled. At any moment, there might be a majority in favour of abolition. When the moment came, when a 49 per cent minority was converted overnight into a 51 per cent majority, what was the Member who had followed Lord Salisbury's advice to do? Change his vote and change his mind? Or change his vote without changing his mind? Or change neither his mind nor his vote? Of course, no swing of opinion was likely to come about with such dramatic suddenness, nor would it be so accurately measurable if it did. But in general terms, this problem was a very real one. If a Member tied himself strictly to the majority opinion in his constituency, the time would come when he would have to vote in the opposite lobby, for no better reason than that he guessed that a slight majority in his constituency now required him to do so.

It seemed to me that this was a jejune approach to a matter of principle. I preferred to be guided by the *trend* of public opinion, in the country as a whole, and particularly in my own constituency; secondly, by the views I heard expressed in Parliament; and thirdly, by my study of all the available evidence. If Silverman succeeded in obtaining a majority for his Bill in the House of Commons, and the House of Lords endorsed it, then Parliament would only be anticipating the public's will by a few years. So, throughout 1955 and the early part of 1956, I consistently voted abolitionist.

In October I modified my attitude. All the other Conservative abolitionists eventually did the same, but as I happened to be the first to do so publicly, and had seconded the Third Reading of Silverman's Bill, I incurred a large share of the reproaches which the Labour Party, and the abolitionists outside Parliament, aimed at us collectively. 'In the eyes of history,' said Anthony Greenwood, 'the credit for the abolition of capital punishment will go to Sydney Silverman and those of his colleagues, who, *in spite of the fact that they were deserted and betrayed by the Conservative abolitionists in Parliament*, continued to fight for the things in which they believed.'[1]

There were several reasons for our decision. After the Lords' rejection of the Silverman Bill, the controversy was bound to drag on for another year, until the Bill could be re-presented in its same form and passed through Parliament against the wishes of the Lords, who would no longer be able to enforce their veto. This year was a dangerous one for the country at home and abroad. The Conservative Party had been split and weakened by the controversy. If we were able to settle it by some compromise measure, backed by the Government, and meeting the abolitionist case halfway, unity would be restored, something practical would have been gained, and the principle itself would not have been abandoned.

In the second place, it was clear that the public needed proof, other than the experience of foreign countries, that abolition would not be followed by the disastrous rise in the murder-rate which they feared. The onus of proof was on the reformers, and they could not provide it, except by making the reform, and waiting to see what happened. There can never be any absolute proof that the substitution of life-imprisonment for hanging will not give murderers a freer rein. Even if the murder-rate were to sink after abolition to one murder a year, it could be said that the one murderer might have been deterred if the death penalty had still been the law. If in opposition to majority public opinion and the advice of the police, total abolition had been forced through Parliament, and the experiment had failed, it would be said that the abolitionists had recklessly gambled away human lives. It is true that whenever a nation have abolished the death-sentence, there has been an element of risk in their decision. Nobody could claim to be certain that the experiment would succeed; he could only claim that its failure was most improbable.

[1] *Hansard*, vol. 564, col. 467. February 6th, 1957.

In those circumstances, it was preferable that the responsibility should be shared by the Government and a large part of the nation.

We had not convinced a majority in the country that the risk was worth taking. Therefore, we must give them the only proof possible, by abolishing the death sentence for some forms of murder and not for others, and judge by the results whether it was safe to proceed to total abolition. The Conservative Conference, which howled down the abolitionist speakers, had been prepared to accept such a limited experiment. If they could be won over by the success of it, we could proceed as a united party to the next stage. It was perhaps better to approach total abolition in two steps with public approval, than in one step without it.

It was therefore with some relief that many Conservatives heard privately in the autumn of 1956 that the Government intended to introduce a measure of this kind, which conceded more than half the abolitionist case. I accordingly told the chairman of my constituency Association, Major Grant, in response to his renewed appeal to abandon my abolitionist stand, that if the Government were to introduce a Bill of this type, I would support it and vote against any amendment to make abolition complete. A few days later I made my pledge public. Inevitably it was said that I had changed my mind. I protested that I had not done so, that I was still as strongly in favour of abolition as ever before. I was glad that our debates in Parliament had reconciled everybody to accepting a change in the law of murder and a limitation on the types of murder for which the death sentence could be imposed. But as I could not be certain that I was right in my forecast about the effect of total abolition, which involved an admitted risk to human lives, and as so large a number of my constituents felt certain that I was wrong, I would support this half-way measure in the hope that they would be convinced by its results.[1]

[1] Since the Homicide Act became law in March 1957, there has been no increase in the murder-rate. 'There was a small increase in April, May and June of 1957, but the figures have fallen since then, and the average is not higher than the average before. The figures for September 1957 to March 1958, were lower than for the same period in 1954 and 1955.' Miss Hornsby-Smith, Under Secretary, Home Office, addressing the Conservative Women's Conference, May 21st, 1958.

In retrospect, I find it difficult to decide whether I was right or wrong to make this compromise. It would be untrue to deny that one of my motives was to make peace with my constituents. They held their views with the same intensity as I held mine. It was a question of balancing their fears of the murderer behind 'the frail latch' against my conviction that hanging was not only barbarous but unnecessary. I had, to a small degree, the power to decide: they had none. If I had continued to oppose their wishes, as the only Conservative Member to do so, I would have deeply shocked them. Up to that moment it had been a matter of argument between us. Now we were approaching the final decision. In the Homicide Bill there was common ground where we could all pause for reflection. I seized the opportunity.

Chapter Five

SUEZ

Whole truth is not yet known—need for discretion—Conservatives' conflict between loyalty and convictions—first reactions to nationalization of Canal—attempts to negotiate with Nasser—the threat to use force—foreign reaction to this threat—Labour reaction—the Canal as a British life-line—Conservative reaction inside and outside Parliament—misgivings of some Conservatives—the case for economic action against Nasser—the Israeli attack—Tripartite Declaration—my talks in Jerusalem—failure to warn Israel—the ultimatum of October 30th—anger of the Americans—was the police-action a pretext for seizing the Canal?—my own reasons for opposing Suez policy—division of public opinion—Conservative support for Sir Anthony Eden—I hesitate to criticize him publicly—probable constituency reactions—Conservative abstentions from vote of confidence.

THE WHOLE TRUTH may never be known about the Suez crisis of the summer and autumn of 1956. It is certainly not known now. Although the crisis aroused more comment and deeper emotions than any other political event since the end of the second world war, there are many questions still unanswered. What was the degree of opposition to Sir Anthony Eden within his own Cabinet? How much, if any, foreknowledge of the Israeli invasion of Sinai did the British or the French Government have? Did the Americans threaten us with economic sanctions unless we withdrew our troops from the Canal? What was the evidence for a Russian plot to create a vast Arab satellite empire? Some of these questions may never be answered, either because records were not taken or because they have since been destroyed; or because the few men who know the answers will not wish to publish them, out of respect for colleagues and allies. There is a real danger that the history of Suez may thus be falsified by the suppression of evidence. In the life-time of the chief participants revelations of this kind may be too inflammatory; after their death it will be too late.

The same limitation applies today to anyone in the Civil Service, the armed forces, or in Parliament, who was even remotely concerned with the events. Every Member of Parliament, certainly on the Government side, knew a little more about them than the

general public, even if it was only their awareness of how private
opinion was moving at Westminster. Some, from their friendship with leading Ministers or chance hints dropped in a party
committee or the smoking-room, knew a good deal more. For
them to betray the confidences of two years ago, while the whole
incident is still politically explosive, would be unforgivable. I
shall not be the first to do so. But one of the lessons of the Suez
crisis is that a Member does acquire, and is expected to acquire,
this extra private information by his daily presence at the centre
of events, and he is quite properly influenced by what he hears
and cannot repeat. If, therefore, he comes to conclusions of which
his constituents disapprove, he cannot make his full case publicly.
He is as much impeded by discretion as he would be by a stammer.

For some Members the crisis raised in an acute form a conflict
between loyalty to their party leaders and their conviction that
their leaders had made a grave error of judgement. The dilemma
was not confined to a single party: it affected all three, Conservative, Labour and Liberal. It arose at a moment when the country
was in great danger, when the armed forces were in action, and
when world opinion was against us. If ever there was a moment
when a political leader, particularly one who was also Prime
Minister, needed the support of all his countrymen inside and
outside Parliament, it was in November, 1956. But just because
the issues were so fundamental, and a second mistake on top of
the first might have plunged us into disaster, every Member was
obliged to consider his own attitude with the greatest care. Before
daring to express his dissent publicly, a Government back-bench
Member must be able to answer affirmatively five questions:
First, did I warn the Government and my constituents of what my
attitude was likely to be? Second, have the Government caught
us unawares by taking a sudden decision which does not develop
logically out of their previous decisions? Third, have I enough
information on which to judge? Fourth, can I truly say that the
Government's action is inconsistent with any of the party's basic
policies and principles? Finally, would my public protest do more
good than harm to the country? It is in the light of these questions
that the attitude of the Conservative opponents of the Suez policy
can best be understood.

When Colonel Nasser announced on July 26th, 1956, at the end of a bitterly anti-Western speech at Alexandria, that his police were at that very moment seizing the key installations of the Suez Canal Company, the anger aroused in Britain was violent and unanimous. Mr Gaitskell said: 'It is all very familiar. It is exactly the same as we encountered from Hitler and Mussolini.'[1] At first it was generally assumed that Nasser had broken a treaty, as Hitler had done by his occupation of the Rhineland in 1936. When it was realized that the 1888 Convention said nothing specifically about the ownership of the Canal, but only referred to 'a definite system destined to guarantee for all times and for all Powers, the free use of the Suez Maritime Canal', anger was in no way abated. 'No British Government,' said the *Daily Herald* on August 2nd, 'can resign itself to Colonel Nasser's being in sole control of a vital British Commonwealth life-line.' It had been agreed by Nasser himself as recently as 1954 that the international character of the Canal should be maintained in accordance with the 1888 Convention, and his action was a complete violation of the spirit, if not the letter, of his undertaking. But it was not so much what he did, as his method of doing it, which united this country against him. It was a dictator's typical gesture of defiance, a *quid pro quo* for his disappointment in failing to tempt the American and British Governments to invest in his project for an Aswan Dam, a highwayman's exploitation of the geographical accident that the isthmus of Suez lay in Egyptian territory. All this, and much more, was said by spokesmen of all political parties during the first days of August. It was an act of robbery which the British nation, and most of their western allies, were not prepared to accept with a mere protest.

But how were we to reverse it? There were four methods open to us: legal action; negotiation with Nasser; economic pressure; or war. The first was scarcely considered, as our legal case, divorced from the political, economic and strategic implications of Nasser's act of nationalization, was by itself not strong enough. The other three were all tried in turn, with varying degrees of urgency, and all failed.

The British Government's intention was clearly stated by Sir

[1] *Hansard*, vol. 557, col. 1613. August 2nd, 1956.

Anthony Eden to the House of Commons on July 30th. 'No arrangements for the future of this great international waterway could be acceptable to Her Majesty's Government which would leave it in the unfettered control of a single power which could, as recent events have shown, exploit it purely for purposes of national policy.'[1] We were thus committed from the start to a conflict with Nasser, from which either he or we would emerge discredited. But in the early stages of the controversy, we made it as easy as possible for him to climb down. Few people noticed that although the act of nationalization was condemned, it was never formally challenged. The proposals of the first London Conference, which Mr Menzies took to Cairo on September 3rd on behalf of the eighteen Powers, recognized the Suez Canal as 'an integral part of Egypt', and at no stage of the long negotiations was it ever suggested that the old Suez Canal Company should regain its monopoly or executive power of control. All that we demanded was full compensation for its shareholders, which Nasser himself had offered in his Alexandria speech without indicating how the money was to be found. It was proposed that the Company should be replaced by a Suez Canal Board, on which Egypt herself would be represented, to operate and develop the Canal, but not to own it. Egypt would be the only power to derive a profit from its undertakings. This proposal was turned down by Nasser on the grounds that 'anything less than full Egyptian operational control of the Canal would be an affront to Egypt.' A later western proposal to set up a Suez Canal Users' Association with which Egypt would be invited to co-operate, likewise met with no success. It was vetoed by Russia and Yugoslavia at the Security Council on October 13th, and Nasser never even troubled formally to reject the suggestion. He stood firm on his legal rights, on the support of the Afro-Asian group of nations, and on his claim, which was later shown to be justified, that Egypt was quite capable of operating the Canal by herself. There was no question, he said, of Egypt closing the Canal to its users, for it was obviously in her own interests to keep it open. He had not violated the 1888 Convention, and had no intention of doing so.

[1] *Hansard*, vol. 557, col. 919. July 30th, 1956.

Sir Anthony Eden, and the French Socialist Prime Minister, M. Guy Mollet, insisted that an Egyptian guarantee to keep the Canal open, and proof that Egypt was able to run it efficiently, were not enough to satisfy them. They had the backing of the United States and all the main users of the Canal in pursuing their diplomatic attempts to force Nasser to accept some form of international operational control. It may seem a small point of difference, when Nasser (who had been in military command of the Canal Zone since the evacuation of the last British troops earlier in the summer) could have closed the Canal at will, Board or no Board. But the whole British and French people felt that they had suffered an affront which they wished to see redressed, not only for the sake of the security of the Canal, but because, as Mr Gaitskell put it on August 2nd, 'if Nasser's prestige is put up sufficiently and ours is put down sufficiently, the effect in that part of the world will be that our friends will desert us because they think we are lost, and go over to Egypt.' The only question which remained, and which came to divide Parliament, the country, and eventually the whole world, in bitter recriminations, was whether we were justified in imposing our will on Egypt by force, if negotiation and pressure of international opinion failed.

The possible use of force was mentioned by Britain and France at all but the very earliest stages of the controversy. The idea appeared first in the London and Paris newspapers on August 3rd with an emphasis that suggested official inspiration. 'If no unanimous agreement has been reached by the end of the time limit,' the *Daily Telegraph* commented, 'Britain and France will feel called on to act to impose whatever solution has been agreed to by a majority' of the London Conference. On the same day the French press spoke of 'a determination to use force if peaceful means failed to persuade Nasser to accept international control'. Unofficial hints of the same sort continued throughout August, simultaneously with the build-up of Anglo-French forces in Malta and Cyprus 'to strengthen our ability to deal with any situation that might arise'.[1] On September 12th, when the House of Commons reassembled for an emergency session, the Prime Minister went a step further. Having described the purpose of the

[1] Sir Anthony Eden. Broadcast. August 8th, 1956.

Suez Canal Users' Association, he declared that if Egypt tried to interfere with the Association or refused to co-operate with it, they would be in breach of the 1888 Convention. He continued: 'In that event, the British Government and others concerned will be free to take such further steps as seem to be required, either through the United Nations, or by other means, for the assertion of their rights.'[1] There was an immediate outcry from the Labour benches: 'What other means?' But the answer was left to be inferred. On September 24th Mr Selwyn Lloyd repeated the words, 'Force will only be used as a last resort'; and at the Conservative Party Conference on October 11th, Anthony Nutting stated on behalf of the Government, 'If the United Nations were to find itself unable to do its duty. . . . I do not believe this country will flinch from it.'

Nobody could therefore complain that the Government did not give warning that if all else failed, they would consider shooting their way into Egypt to impose a solution. It was clear from the context of these warnings that Sir Anthony and M. Mollet were not merely thinking of attacking Nasser in self-defence, if for instance he prevented ships from passing peacefully through the Canal, or if he imprisoned British and French nationals in Cairo. Nor did they bind themselves to refrain from using force until they had obtained the sanction of the United Nations. It was a plain threat to act unilaterally and without further provocation from Nasser, and it contrasted strongly with the patient and reasonable proposals which they were simultaneously putting to Egypt through the Canal users' conferences and the Security Council.

If the world was left in no doubt that the British and French Governments had these ultimate measures in mind, nor were the two Governments left in any doubt about world reaction to them. It was quite clear from mid-September onwards, in spite of some earlier equivocations, that the United States would not associate herself in any way with such a policy. On September 13th, Mr Dulles declared that if Egypt refused to co-operate with the Users' Association, which had first been suggested by him, no American ship would be allowed to shoot its way through the

[1] *Hansard*, vol. 558, col. 11. September 12th, 1956.

Canal, but would be diverted round the Cape. He regarded the affair as a matter for hard bargaining with a tough and wholly unreliable political buccaneer: the British and French Prime Ministers regarded it as an already warlike situation. The difference between their two approaches became more evident every day.

The same was true of Western Europe. The Scandinavian countries were at first unwilling to attend the second London Conference for fear of becoming involved in Anglo-French manœuvres which they considered to be dangerously bellicose. The Italians and West Germans were known to be uneasy. The Asian nations among the eighteen Powers were even more so. As early as August 8th, Nehru had said, 'Threats to settle this dispute by the display or use of force are the wrong way. It does not belong to this age, and is not dictated by reason.' Canada, Australia and New Zealand wanted to help us, but in the main they seemed to share the American view. On September 26th, Mr Menzies spoke for them all in suggesting, 'Nasser must be brought to understand that his course of action is unprofitable to his people *by diverting revenues from Egypt.*' (My italics.)

Simultaneously, and with far greater emphasis, the Labour and Liberal opposition parties in Britain were warning the Prime Minister that he could not count on their support for an act of war to solve the crisis. From left-wing Socialists there had been criticism of the tone of Mr Gaitskell's speech on August 2nd, which they considered to be too sympathetic to the Government's precautionary troop-movements, but Mr Gaitskell had safe-guarded himself by adding:

But we must act in concert with other nations. . . . Obviously there are circumstances in which we might be compelled to use force, in self-defence or as a part of some collective defence measures. . . . I must however remind the House that we are signatories to the United Nations Charter, and that for many years we have steadfastly avoided any international action which would be in breach of international law, or indeed contrary to the public opinion of the world. We must not therefore allow ourselves to get into a position where we might be denounced in the Security Council as aggressors, or where the majority of the Assembly were against us.[1]

[1] *Hansard,* vol. 557, cols. 1616–17. August 2nd, 1956.

These warnings were repeated by Labour leaders almost weekly until the end of October, by letters to the press, speeches in Parliament, and personal interviews with the Prime Minister. The TUC at their conference in early September and the Labour Party Conference at Blackpool on October 1st, endorsed their point-of-view. There was no doubt that a war with Nasser to enforce internationalization of the Canal would not be supported by millions of Englishmen, unless it were approved by the United Nations in advance. Their attitude may have been thought supine, but it was at least clear.

Why, then, did Sir Anthony Eden, in face of this evidence from at home and abroad, persist in his threat, and eventual decision, to use force? For two basic reasons; because he considered that our very existence as a great Power could in the last resort be upheld in no other way; and because of the demand within his own party for strong and effective action.

His speeches returned again and again to the theme of Hitler and the Munich crisis. He had resigned the Foreign Secretaryship in 1938, six months before Munich, in protest against Chamberlain's weakness towards the dictators. He was not going to make the same mistake himself. If Nasser were allowed to achieve without penalty the nationalizing of the Canal, he would advance by stages to complete mastery of the Middle East. But, in Sir Anthony's view, Nasser's action was not only a warning of what was likely to follow unless he were immediately checked; it was in itself 'a matter of life and death to us all', as he said in his broadcast of August 8th. 'If Colonel Nasser's action were to succeed, each one of us would be at the mercy of one man for the supplies upon which we live.' The Canal might have lost its old strategic importance as a military route to the eastern half of the British Empire. But it had gained an even greater importance as the channel by which the major part of our oil-supplies reached us from the Persian Gulf. It was the possibility that this route might suddenly be closed that appalled the Prime Minister. He did not consider that we should wait until Nasser gave us a further excuse to intervene. He had given us excuse enough already, and if the rest of the world and the British Labour Party did not think so, theirs was not the ultimate responsibility. 'No arrangements,' he had said on July 30th, 'could be acceptable to us which would leave the Canal in the unfettered control of a single power.' That was a pledge to the country, and above all to his own party, from which there was no escaping. In one way or another it must be honoured.

It was emphatically endorsed by Conservatives in and out of Parliament. There had been a mounting feeling of regret that we had agreed in 1954 to withdraw British troops from the Canal Zone. Although when we still had 80,000 men on the Canal, there had been little or no demand to enforce the 1951 resolution of the United Nations to permit Israeli ships to have free passage in accordance with the 1888 Convention, it was now considered with some reason that Nasser would never have dared to carry out his act of nationalization if he had had to contend with a British army on the spot. Those twenty or thirty members of the Parliamentary party, headed by Captain Charles Waterhouse and Mr Julian Amery, who had loudly protested at the time against our evacuation, were now held to have been justified by events. No matter that our continued occupation of the Zone against the wishes of Egypt would have exposed us to constant misrepresentation and a growing terrorist campaign, which would have nullified the purpose of a base designed to serve the whole Middle East. The fact remained that Egypt had acted within a few months of the departure of the last British soldier. It was a double insult. Our position must be regained. There was little difference in Conservative eyes between Nasser's seizure of the Canal, and the violation of a frontier. 'He will not be argued out of it simply by reason,' said Mr Walter Elliot on August 2nd. 'There is a moment when he has to be withstood, and that moment is here.' He was undoubtedly expressing the dominant mood of Conservatives in Parliament.

Among Conservatives outside Parliament the demand for action was even more unmistakable. Nobody can fully understand the Suez crisis unless he takes into account their growing unease that Britain's position in the world, and the reputation of the Conservative Government at home, were being whittled down through lack of strong leadership. They saw evidence of weakness in the Government's handling of the Trades Unions, in the constant increase in the cost-of-living, in the controversy over capital punishment, in the worsening situation in Cyprus. A by-election at Tonbridge in the early summer had shown a big drop in the Conservative majority, due largely, it was thought, to these causes. If Sir Winston Churchill were still Prime Minister, it was widely and most unfairly said, these troubles would have been solved overnight. The one moment when Conservative spirits rose was when Archbishop Makarios was deported from Cyprus to the Seychelles in March, 1956. I shall not forget the surge of approval which greeted me when I announced the news to a Conservative meeting in my own constituency. I fully understood their emotion. It was not blind jingoism, nor merely an instinctive dislike of any foreign troublemaker. It was a sense of relief that we had at last done something to check decline. It was the gesture, as much as the reasons for it, that stirred them. When Nasser nationalized the Canal, a similar gesture was looked for, and promised.

The possible alternatives to military action were regarded with suspicion and some impatience by most Conservatives. If the ultimatum to Egypt, even without the pretext of an Israeli invasion or previous reference of the dispute to the United Nations, had been presented during the first days of August or in early September, Sir Anthony Eden would have had their overwhelming support. His attempts to negotiate with Nasser and the debate on the Security Council were regarded by many as little more than the stylized preliminaries to inevitable combat. They could see no satisfactory end to these discussions. With every week that passed, Nasser's hand was strengthened by the increasing unwillingness of international shipping to deny themselves the use of the Canal on almost any terms that Egypt cared to offer. The United Nations had again and again demonstrated its ineffectiveness. Its few successes in the political field, such as in Korea, had been achieved through a combination of good luck and the energy with which a single member-nation had acted without waiting for formal permission. Even if it passed a resolution condemning Nasser, who was to enforce it? It had not a single soldier at its disposal. And what chance was there of a polyglot Assembly agreeing by a sufficient majority to permit Britain and France to re-establish their rights by force, although nearly all its members stood to benefit by the result?

These emotions reached a climax at the Conservative Party Conference on October 11th. Resolutions had poured in demanding 'firm and clear leadership' and 'a more vigorous Conservative policy'. The emphasis was on leading the nation instead of nursing it, and it was soon evident that the delegates had in mind the Egyptian situation as much as our domestic problems. One of them referred to the Opposition's attack on the Prime Minister for his reservations about the possible use of force, as 'the most treacherous action of any major political party'. The conference rose to Julian Amery when he said, 'If the discussions at the Security Council do not bring Nasser to his senses, I believe the process of negotiation will then be exhausted. . . . Our hands will be free to use any and every measure which may be necessary to achieve our ends, including if necessary the use of force. We must go forward with the Americans' approval if we can get it, without it if they withhold it, and against their wishes if needs be.'[1]

When I read these words in the aircraft on my way to Strasbourg, and heard in my mind the tumultuous cheering which accompanied them, my blood ran cold.

It is impossible to know how far Sir Anthony Eden's judgement was influenced by these demonstrations. It was my impression at the time that they alarmed him. He had an unqualified mandate from the great bulk of his party, and even, as it later appeared, from many Labour supporters in the country, to go to extreme lengths if he could not reach a solution by peaceful means. But the mandate was turning imperceptibly into an instruction, which he could only ignore at great peril. The mood of the party was duplicated by the mood of the whole of France. This double pressure must have weighed heavily against his natural inclination to avoid at all costs, even at the cost of personal and national humiliation, a breach with our major allies and the Commonwealth. 'I think we should be doing Sir Anthony a disservice,' I said in a constituency speech on September 26th, 'if by infectious enthusiasm for dealing with Nasser in the toughest possible way, we should drive the Prime Minister into a position from which

[1] *The Times*. October 12th, 1956.

the only escape is through a last-minute climb-down or by an
unpopular and costly war.' I repeated the same idea in a letter to
the *Sunday Times*, elaborating the reasons why I thought that a
solution by force was the worst of all solutions. There was a nasty
editorial note printed at the foot of my letter: 'Mr Nicolson cannot always be available for consultation by responsible Ministers,
to whom he should really give credit for being as well aware as
he is of these considerations.' Perhaps I had been too arrogant.
The snub may well have been deserved. But a month later the
Prime Minister had been driven into precisely this position, which
surely he, too, must have feared.

Considerable blame for what later happened must attach to us,
the Conservatives who felt strongly that the party was losing its
head, for not expressing our point-of-view with enough clarity
or cogency. At the opening of the emergency session of Parliament
on September 12th, *The Times* lobby correspondent could write;
'Among Conservative supporters there was not even a whiff of
criticism of the Government,' when there was already much
anxiety on the back benches that we were heading for a situation
which would become increasingly out of control. Those of us
who felt like this were quite unorganized. We barely knew each
other's identity. The Suez Group continued to dominate the party
committees. For one moment it seemed that Sir Lionel Heald,
an ex-Attorney General, might emerge as our natural leader. But
it soon became clear that he did not share our worst fears. He
merely sounded a note of warning on the question of submitting
the dispute to the United Nations. In the second day's debate, he
read out the Articles of the United Nations' Charter which defined
the circumstances under which a nation might legitimately
take matters into its own hands, and continued, 'There is a clear
obligation, before resort is had to force, that the matter should be
referred to the Security Council. . . . If a reasonable and proper
plan is approved there, then I personally will be willing to support
the Government in any measure they then think it necessary to
carry out.'[1] But if no plan was approved, or if no authority was
given by the United Nations to execute an approved plan when
diplomatic methods had failed, what was to be our position? This

[1] *Hansard*, vol. 558, col. 184. September 13th, 1956.

was the question which the debate left unanswered. Most Members, even on the Labour side, were understandably reluctant to press for an answer, after the Prime Minister had agreed, as a first step, to appeal to the United Nations, because the answer would have told Nasser what he most wished to know. But the ambiguity made it inevitable that when an answer was finally given, by the ultimatum on October 30th, it would come with numbing suddenness.

There can be little doubt that the Whips and Cabinet were well aware that a small minority of the parliamentary party would oppose a unilateral resort to force, even if their voices were almost drowned inside Parliament by the Suez Group, and outside were scarcely heard at all. Non-parliamentary comment was more vocal. *The Times* and *Manchester Guardian* carried on a duel with leading articles, the former supporting with increasing hesitation a policy of 'a foot in the door', the latter standing up consistently for a policy based on international law and morality. The Archbishop of Canterbury told the country in September that 'the decision must be such as to command the general assent of all parties and of the whole nation', and the United Nations Association added their own warnings. But in general the presentation of the case against the use of force in any circumstances except in self-defence was left to the spokesmen for the Labour and Liberal Parties. Their solution rested on maintaining the authority of the United Nations. They had less to say on what our action should be if the United Nations failed us. They never explored in enough detail the possibilities of economic action against Nasser, by which he might have been deprived of the fruits of his robbery much more effectively than by war.

The case for economic action was best put, retrospectively, by a member of the Government, Lord Home, the Secretary of State for Commonwealth Relations. He had no remorse about the ultimatum of October 1956. But seven months later, in what he hoped was 'the last of the post-mortems' on the Suez crisis, he considered the possible alternatives for the future. In his opinion, there were only two: an international agreement, such as was originally proposed by the eighteen Powers, and which he considered we would be unlikely to achieve in Nasser's present mood;

or a policy to 'minimize our dependence on the Canal'. He continued:

We must do so by all the means in our power: by new pipelines; by new and larger tankers, for which plans are well under way; by increasing our capacity to produce more steel; by increasing stockpiling of oil in this country and on the continent of Europe; and by stepping up the search for oil, and for this there is certainly scope in Canada, in North Africa, including Libya, in Latin America and in Europe itself. . . . If Colonel Nasser prefers to play politics, then the Canal will inevitably dwindle in stature and performance into an insignificant local waterway.[1]

Nasser had played politics in July 1956, and this could have been his answer then. I thought so in September of that year, and I still think so today. His objects in seizing the Canal were prestige and money. We could have deprived him of both. We could have made the Canal a liability to Egypt instead of her main asset; for while we often spoke of the Canal as our jugular vein, we were apt to forget that it was also Egypt's. We could have used it decreasingly, and gradually replaced the oil by the methods which Lord Home later suggested. We could have maintained our hold on Egypt's overseas assets, used them to compensate the Canal Company's shareholders, and cut to the minimum the trade we carried on with her. It would mean some loss to us in foreign currency, and a slight temporary rise in our cost-of-living. But our sacrifice would be nothing compared with Egypt's, and nothing compared to the sacrifices involved in a Middle East war. We would have kept open our offer to resume full use of the Canal as soon as Nasser agreed to the eighteen Power plan, but we should not meanwhile have relaxed our efforts to by-pass it. It would have taken time for the policy to be fully effective; but its purpose would have been clear from the start. Nasser would have found himself with a half-empty suitcase instead of a bag of gold. It would have been a classic demonstration to the world, and particularly to the Arab States, of the power of economic pressure against a Government which dishonours its agreements and throws away a valuable monopoly.

[1] *Hansard*, House of Lords, vol. 203, cols. 1170-1. May 23rd, 1957.

At the same time, we could have blocked Nasser's future plans for expanding his empire. We knew exactly what he hoped to do. He wished to lead an Arab crusade to obliterate Israel; to annex the Sudan, and reach out towards central Africa. He planned to stop ships from passing through the Canal whenever he was displeased, and to hold valuable cargoes to ransom. Until July 1956, there had not been the unity or determination in the West to give him clear warning of the consequences of gratifying his ambitions. Now, nearly every country, incensed by Nasser's actions, was in the mood to give him that warning. A pact could have been negotiated with the United States, France and other western European countries, or if necessary between France and ourselves alone, to make it clear beyond doubt that if Nasser stopped our ships, seized our military installations at Suez, or attacked his neighbours, he would do so at the risk of war with the West.

These ideas were not my own. They were evolved in many discussions with many people during those summer months. They were shared by many Conservatives. I put them forward in a series of constituency speeches during late September and early October, 1956.[1] They were well received. I had sent the chairman of my Association, Major Grant, a summary of what I intended to say, and he had found no fault with it. When the Anglo-French ultimatum was delivered a few weeks later, all this was forgotten. We were told that our intervention had nothing to do with the three-month-old quarrel with Nasser. It was a police-action to separate the Egyptian army from the invading army of Israel.

Thus for the first time, on October 29th, 1956, whether by intention or not, the two central problems of the Middle East— the problem of the Suez Canal, and the problem of Jewish-Arab hostility—were fused into one. Up till that moment the only direct link between them had been the refusal of Egypt to allow Israeli shipping to use the Canal, and her defiance of the United Nations' condemnation of that embargo. To this the western powers had reluctantly turned a blind eye. It was certainly one of Israel's war aims to open the Canal to her shipping, and one of

[1] See *Bournemouth Daily Echo*. September 27th, 1956.

the few which she did not achieve. But of much more importance to her was the freeing of the Straits of Tiran at the entrance to the Gulf of Aqaba from Egyptian domination. In this she was success-ful. Neither aim was openly admitted by Britain or France to be a legitimate excuse for war. They were regarded as two of several forms of Egyptian provocation of Israel which mitigated Ben-Gurion's offence without wholly excusing it. Both he and Nasser were equally guilty, the former of aggression, the latter of pro-voking it. The police action was designed to break up the brawl before it became a danger to the whole area.

The situation was, however, a good deal more complicated than this explanation suggested. Since May 1950 the Tripartite Declaration signed by Britain, France and the United States, had bound the three powers to come to the aid of Israel or of any of the Arab countries should one side be attacked by the other. The wording of this part of the Declaration was as follows:

The three Governments, should they find that any of these States was preparing to violate frontiers or armistice lines, would, consistently with their obligations as Members of the United Nations, immediately take action, both within and outside the United Nations, to prevent such violation.

Repeatedly during the years following the signature of this Declaration, all three governments had reaffirmed it. 'I know very few international instruments, if any,' Sir Anthony Eden had told the House of Commons in November, 1954, 'which carry as strong a commitment as that one does. . . . Do the terms of the 1950 Declaration bind us to go to the help of Israel if she is attacked by an Arab State? The answer is, yes, most certainly. They not only bind us, but they bind the United States and France also, in exactly the same way, whether it be Israel or an Arab state.'[1] At intervals during the first half of 1956 this assurance was repeated nine times by British Government spokesmen. It seemed that no clearer warning could have been given to Israel or her Arab neighbours that any renewal of hostilities between them would bring down the overwhelming force of the West on the side of the victim of attack.

[1] *Hansard*, vol. 532, col. 326. November 2nd, 1954.

The Tripartite Declaration was well known to all Members of Parliament but unfamiliar to the great majority of their constituents. No attempt had been made to conceal the seriousness of the obligations it imposed on us; quite the contrary. But it scarcely occurred to the average Englishman between 1950 and 1956 that at any moment his country might be involved in a major campaign on the side either of the Jews or of the Arabs. Thus when at the height of the Suez crisis the Declaration was suddenly said to be inapplicable to the case of an Israeli attack on Egypt, few people outside Parliament were as startled as they would undoubtedly have been if the Treaty had suddenly been invoked by Egypt following an attack on her territory by Israel. I had always thought that there was danger in this public unawareness of the Declaration, and I took every opportunity to refer to it. I emphasized that it was the best safeguard of peace in the Middle East, provided that Jew and Arab were equally convinced that the three Western Powers meant what they said, and that the peoples of our three countries knew and approved of the responsibilities which their governments had undertaken in their name.

Unfortunately neither Jew nor Arab was convinced. When I mentioned the Declaration to the Israeli Prime Minister, Mr Moshe Sharett, at an interview in Jerusalem in April, 1955, he almost laughed. 'Look,' I said, showing him the official report of Sir Anthony's statement in the House five months before. 'Nothing could be more categorical than that. Why don't you believe it?' He gave me five reasons, which I noted down immediately afterwards. The Declaration, he said, has already been broken by supplying arms unilaterally to Jordan and Iraq; Eden's statement is not fully binding, since it was merely made in answer to a chance parliamentary question; the British Government has consistently refused to embark on diplomatic or staff talks to work out the actual methods by which help could be brought to Israel if she were to be attacked; the French and the Americans have been very lukewarm about the Declaration; and, finally, on another occasion Eden has hinted that his pledge depended on a settlement of Israel's dispute with the Arabs.

There were answers to all these objections, and I gave them. I said that it was inconceivable that a British Foreign Secretary could give so firm an undertaking, and later dishonour it. Mr Sharett was still not convinced. I returned to London alarmed by the implications of what I had heard. If Israel considered that she could attack her neighbours with impunity, she would be likely to do so, because she knew that she could defeat them all single-handed, and because if she did not do so, she was risking an attack on herself. Correspondingly, if the Arab leaders held the same views as Mr Sharett about the meaninglessness of the Tripartite Declaration, they would be much more tempted to launch a surprise attack on Israel. The uncertainty of allied intentions in the minds of both sides greatly increased the risks of war.

Anglo-American conversations in Washington in the early part of 1956 did little to instil greater confidence in the Declaration. While all three western Governments repeatedly asserted that the Declaration meant what it said, the Americans were prohibited by their constitution from giving any more precise definition of their intentions or engaging in staff talks with either side in the Middle East. British and French troops in the Mediterranean were already fully occupied with Cyprus and Algeria. It seemed that even if the allies had the will to implement the Declaration, they had not the means to do so. Only when Anglo-French reinforcements were rushed to Cyprus in August to meet Nasser's threat, was the Declaration accidentally given strength. The same troops could be used either to counter any new move by Nasser, or to intervene in an Arab-Jewish war on the side of the victim of attack. The American Sixth Fleet was also in the Mediterranean, available to complete the partnership. As this was a period of mounting tension between Israel and Jordan, and between Israel and Egypt, it seemed a suitable moment to remind both sides that open hostilities between them would lead to allied intervention in force. Such a warning was given by Britain to Mr Ben-Gurion, now once again Prime Minister of Israel, but it referred only to Israeli raids on Jordan. One hundred and sixty people had already been killed in September and October on the Jordanian frontier, and if a major Israeli attack followed, Ben-Gurion was told, we should be obliged to come to Jordan's help, in spite of the recent worsening of Anglo-Jordanian relations, because we were doubly bound to aid her, under the terms of the Anglo-Jordanian Treaty and under the Tripartite Declaration. Nothing so specific was said about an Israeli attack on Egypt.

We could have stopped Israel's attack on Egypt by warning her in advance that such an attack would inevitably involve the three Western Powers against her. If Israel replied that she feared an attack on herself by Egypt, our answer was that the Declaration applied equally to both sides, and the same warning could have been given to Nasser. Both sides knew that at last we had the strength available in the area to implement our threat. We failed to give that warning. In the event, we demonstrated that Mr Sharett's disbelief had been well-founded. For years the Tripartite Declaration had been the key-stone of our Middle East policy. When it came to the moment of decision, it was shown to be porous. We did not do what we had consistently promised to do.

It was worse than that. We failed to inform our major ally and co-signatory, the United States, that we intended to substitute for joint action under the Declaration a surprise ultimatum to both sides, greatly to the disadvantage of Egypt, the immediate victim of attack. It is still not quite certain what happened, but this much has already been revealed. On October 28th, after Israel had announced her partial mobilization, President Eisenhower, then at the height of his presidential election campaign, sent an urgent message to Ben-Gurion expressing grave concern, and warning Israel not to start hostilities. Later on the same day, as reports came in of complete mobilization, he sent a further message. At the same time Mr Dulles called the British and French chargés d'affaires to meet him in Washington to discuss what measures should be taken under the Tripartite Declaration to meet this situation. Next morning, on the 29th, the Israelis attacked. The discussions in Washington were continued on that day, and in the evening the White House issued the following statement:

The United States has pledged itself to assist the victim of any aggression in the Middle East. We shall honour our pledge. The United States is in consultation with the British and French Governments, parties with us to the Tripartite Declaration of 1950, and the United States plans, as contemplated by that Declaration, that the situation shall be taken to the United Nations Security Council tomorrow morning.

The British and French representatives were instructed to join with the United States in calling that meeting. When it met, the discussions were interrupted by the news from London of the Anglo-French ultimatum. Not even the British representative on the Security Council had any foreknowledge of it. The United States certainly had none. At a later meeting of the Security Council that same evening, the British and French vetoes were cast against the American resolution calling on Israel 'immediately to withdraw its armed forces behind the established armistice lines'.

So much is fact. The British Government later stated that it was their impression that the Americans had agreed with us at the Washington meeting of the Tripartite Powers that Egypt had dissociated herself from the Declaration, and it was therefore inapplicable in her defence.[1] However, it appears from the White House statement that the Americans were already considering the possibility of joint action under the Declaration, since it spoke of honouring their pledge 'to assist the victim of *any* aggression in the Middle East.' It was the purpose of the Security Council meeting to discuss what that action should be. We anticipated it by taking a wholly different action, both outside the United Nations and outside the Tripartite Declaration, on which hitherto we had set such store. The Americans could not conceal their anger. 'The United States,' said the President on October 31st, 'was not consulted in any way about any phase of these actions, which can scarcely be reconciled with the principles and purposes of the United Nations.'

I have laid emphasis on this aspect of the Suez crisis because it is relatively unfamiliar, and it strongly affected my own attitude. To me it was symptomatic of the tactless, even cagey, methods with which Great Britain and France treated their major ally. It seemed almost unbelievable that trained diplomatists could rise from their long conference in Washington with utter confusion in their minds about the immediate intentions of their partners. If the White House statement had given an incorrect impression of the decisions arrived at, it could immediately have been corrected. If the United States had agreed with us that the Tripartite Declaration was inapplicable to the situation, why did

[1] *Hansard*, vol. 558, col. 1568. October 31st, 1956.

her Government put such emphasis upon it? If Egypt had told us privately that she had no wish that the Treaty should be invoked in her defence, that was no reason for us to abrogate it. The purpose of the Treaty was to prevent a war spreading, not to defend one side: Egypt's attitude to it was immaterial. It is said that British and French opinion would not have tolerated the sending of troops solely to Nasser's aid, whatever our obligations; there was no need for us to have done so. We could have brought the fighting to a halt by attacking either side which made a further move forward; we could have landed at Gaza instead of at Port Said, for at Gaza an Egyptian garrison was besieged, and it lay on the frontier, the proper point for a neutral intervention. If, finally, it is said that the Americans would not have joined with us in stopping the fighting, we gave them no opportunity to say whether they would or not. If they had not, Britain and France, who proceeded to act unilaterally outside the Declaration, could have intervened together, much more effectively, within it.

It was these considerations, and others, which led me to believe that the purpose of our intervention was not solely to stop the fighting, but also to seize the opportunity to settle our quarrel with Nasser over the Canal, and stifle at birth his further ambitions. The very terms of our ultimatum, which called on Egypt to accept Anglo-French military occupation of the Canal Zone whether the fighting had stopped or not, and included as one of its stated purposes 'to guarantee freedom of transit through the Canal by the ships of all nations', reinforced my belief. I still hold it. Even if such a suspicion was undeserved, we certainly failed to convince the world that it was. It was widely believed in the United States and elsewhere that we had deliberately concealed our plan from the Americans for fear that it would be vetoed by them. To have created a false impression on that scale must be counted among the biggest blunders of British diplomatic history. It so diminished our credit, that millions of people abroad were soon willing to accept without hesitation the even graver charge that Britain, France and Israel had been guilty of collusion.

But was it a false impression? In a remarkable review of the Brombergers' book, *Secrets of Suez*, which appeared in the *Sunday Times* on July 14th, 1957, written anonymously 'by an expert whose intimate knowledge of the events in question assures its authority but equally prevents the publication of his name', the following passage occurred in the course of a passionate defence of the Eden policy:

The British Government sought in vain for months to induce the United States Government to recognize the danger [of Nasser's ambitions]. When they failed, they had two courses open to them: to allow the Russian design and Nasser's plans to unfold and tamely to endure the consequences; or to attempt to check Nasser, if necessary by force—which clearly was a gamble. It was a choice of evils, but when the two Governments [of Britain and France], exasperated by the equivocations of Mr Dulles, eventually decided to act, they certainly did not do so in reliance on help from America. *Otherwise they would presumably have given Washington some advance notice of their intentions.* (My italics.)

This could never have been written eight months earlier without arousing a storm of indignation. As it appeared after the passions created by the Suez crisis had abated, it passed without comment. It is a frank, authoritative admission that the main reason for the Suez action was quite different from the main reason given in October, and that we failed to inform the Americans, not because of lack of time, as we later said, but because we could not rely on their support for an action of which we knew they would disapprove. The Israeli invasion, even if we had no foreknowledge of it until the moment of Ben-Gurion's attack, was seized on as a pretext for invading Egypt from a new direction.

Under two conditions only could our manœuvre possibly have been justified, even on purely tactical grounds; if it was almost certain that the western world would believe us; and if our attack on Egypt was likely to result in Nasser's fall and the immediate decline of Russian influence in the Middle East. Neither condition applied. The world did not believe us. The circumstances and method of our intervention revealed our major purpose all too clearly. Even if it had been pressed home in defiance of world opinion, it could still not have had the result we predicted. 'This almost incredible misjudgement,' as Lord Tedder called it, ended in the humiliation of ourselves, not of Nasser; in the decline of British influence in the Middle East, not of Russia's. Nasser

might have been overthrown by force, but only if we had occupied the whole of Egypt. A puppet Government set up to replace
him could only have survived if our troops had stayed there
indefinitely, a possibility excluded by the ultimatum. We would
have been subjected to guerrilla attack, morally supported by the
United Nations, and physically, perhaps, by Russian volunteers.
The flow of Middle East oil, which was of even greater importance
to us than the Canal, would have been interrupted or diverted.
The United States would have threatened to take economic
measures to force us to halt. All our alliances, NATO, the
Commonwealth, the Baghdad Pact, SEATO, would have been
put under great strain. Half our own countrymen would have
opposed it bitterly, and the army itself would have felt no confidence in its political leadership.

So we halted the operation, just in time. The reasons which
caused us to halt it were precisely the same as those which could
have been foreseen in time to prevent us from embarking upon
it. Britain is not strong or ruthless enough to persist indefinitely
in a policy which shocks her friends. 'Even in a purely practical
sense,' a great British strategist has written, 'it is wiser for Britain
to follow a consistently moral policy, since we have become
incapable of carrying out an amoral policy effectively. The checks
in our democratic system, our moral scruples, and difficulty in
carrying ruthlessness to an extreme, form a triple handicap on
success in power politics.'

So disturbed was our moral balance that we strangely failed to
take any credit for the method by which we soon partially restored
our reputation. We greatly strengthened the authority of the
United Nations by accepting the Assembly's demand on us to
cease fire and withdraw. By that action, which contrasted strongly
with the contemporary behaviour of Russia in Hungary, we
showed what President Eisenhower has called 'a decent respect for
the opinions of mankind.' It was, however, that very action which
aroused the anger of the extreme advocates of the Suez policy. To
halt was bad enough; but to halt at the dictation of the Assembly
was a humiliation which we surely might have been spared. So
arose the legend, among the many legends which the crisis left
behind, of the Assembly's 'double standard of morality'. There

was no double standard: there was only one, the standard which is Britain's own traditional standard. The true difference was that we, in the end, returned to it; the Russians did not.

British opinion was deeply divided, and still is, on the wisdom and morality of our action. Contrary attitudes were taken up with such intensity of feeling that it was difficult to believe that we could be talking about the same set of circumstances. The *Manchester Guardian* called the ultimatum 'an act of folly without justification in any terms but brief expediency'. The *Sunday Times* commented, 'Thanks to the courage of the British and the French, a chance is being created of making a fresh start.' 'For too many years,' wrote a correspondent to the *Observer*, 'the British nation has suffered snubs and insults with loss of prestige and possessions, and today countless Britons are grateful to think the country is at last taking a firm stand.' Public figures as diverse as Sir Winston Churchill, Dr Gilbert Murray, Mr Roy Harrod and the Warden of All Souls, supported the Prime Minister. Mr Harrod wrote, 'I believe that the Government's action, seen in the perspective of a few months from now, will be judged to have been not only right, but a signal and statesmanlike contribution to the aims of the United Nations.' Lady Violet Bonham-Carter felt 'humiliation, shame and anger which are beyond expression.' The Oxford Union voted against the Suez policy by 352 to 206. At Leigh-on-sea, when the vicar of St Clement's told his congregation that Suez was 'an unjust war', several of them walked out of the church, and his Bishop threatened to dispense with his services 'for gross disloyalty to his incumbent'. Lord Russell of Liverpool resigned from the Liberal Party, which he had just joined, in order to support the Prime Minister. While the Archbishop of Canterbury said that 'Christian opinion is terribly uneasy and unhappy', the Bishop of Durham did not share his qualms. He thought the ultimatum 'the highest order of courage. . . . The man in the street was relieved that something had been done, right or wrong, to stop a great evil.'

The Bishop was certainly justified in attributing this feeling to ordinary Conservatives. Their support for Sir Anthony Eden was overwhelming. Telegrams pledging absolute loyalty arrived at

Downing Street in sack-loads. The attacks made on him by the Labour Party and the hostile press were thought to be all the more shocking because our troops were about to go into action and Britain was under heavy criticism from abroad. This was not the way in which Conservatives had expected war to come, and until that moment their sympathy for Israel had been cool. But whatever the immediate causes or likely consequences of our action were, they saw in it the response to their cheers and resolutions at the party conference three weeks before. This was, at last, 'firm and clear leadership.' Nasser—the association between the ultimatum and the old enemy was instinctive—would now be taught a lesson, and the vacillations of the Americans and the United Nations would be exposed.

It is not pleasant to find oneself completely out of sympathy with the dominant mood of one's party, particularly at a moment of great danger and emotion. I felt the Prime Minister's decision to be utterly, utterly wrong. I thought it immoral because it violated one of our party's deepest principles and our country's most honourable traditions; I thought it foolish, because it could not possibly succeed. In the past few years I had many times sat behind Sir Anthony in the House of Commons while he dominated that most difficult assembly by his lucidity, knowledge, high principle and unfailing judgement. How could such a man, I asked myself, now initiate an action which conflicted with every lesson in international relations which I had ever heard him expound? How could those many others in his Cabinet, whose general principles I had come to recognize as magnifications of my own, have consented to be parties to it?

On one of those autumn days, I went late in the evening to the counter in St Stephen's Hall to buy some Christmas cards. The attendant left to fetch them. I was alone in that high chapel where the House of Commons had met for nearly three hundred years. The door at the east end, leading from the central lobby, suddenly opened, and Mr R. A. Butler walked towards me down the steps and across the tiles. He was then acting Prime Minister, after Sir Anthony's departure for Jamaica. We had not spoken since the Suez crisis began. I wondered whether he would speak now. I waited by the bookstall in some embarrassment, for it is a long

walk from one end of the hall to the other, and I felt that the
same thoughts must be in his mind as were in my own. Here was
I, by then a declared opponent of the Suez policy and dubbed a
traitor by my constituents; and there was he, leader of the Government, a party to all its decisions, and an old friend of my family.
What could he possibly say? What could I possibly answer? As
he drew abreast of me, he smiled and slightly inclined his head, and
then passed on through the swing-doors. Not a word was spoken.
I did not know, and do not know, whether he felt that I had been
right or wrong in my opinion, right or wrong to express it.

It was my ignorance of the hidden motives and opinions of the
Cabinet in the midst of all the clamour about the consequences,
that made me hesitate to declare myself. Were there considerations
known only to the Government which would alter my own point-
of-view if I knew them too? If there were, I decided, it could only
be secret information about the extent of Communist penetration
of the Middle East. In that case, President Eisenhower would
have had the same information. We could have consulted him.
It was incomprehensible why we did not do so. The immediate
resignation of Anthony Nutting, Minister of State at the Foreign
Office, where he had been in charge of both the Middle East and
United Nations departments, seemed to confirm my view.

It would have been unforgivable if I had blurted out my
objections at a moment when the troop-convoys were on their
way from Malta to Port Said, and our airmen were risking their
lives nightly over Cairo. There was now no chance that the operation could be halted, and even a single unknown back-bench voice
challenging the Government's action might cause a platoon-
commander momentary annoyance or vague disquiet, if he heard
an echo of it on his radio on the eve of the attack. It was not a risk
worth taking. When the fighting had stopped, I could make my
demonstration without harming anyone but myself. Meanwhile,
I kept my Whips and the chairman of my constituency Association
informed of the action I was contemplating. When required to say
anything in public, I merely stated the reasons which the Government had given for their action, and added nothing, either in
support of them or against them.

I knew that my protest would mean a fierce quarrel with my

constituents. Like all Conservative Associations throughout the country, they were deeply loyal to the Prime Minister and approved wholeheartedly of his decision. When it was announced that Mr Gaitskell was to be allowed to broadcast his reply to the Prime Minister, I received several telegrams from Bournemouth protesting that this decision was outrageous. The country was at war, and the country's leader had the right to expect that he could address the nation without being stabbed in the back a day later. I could therefore guess all too clearly what their reactions would be when their own Conservative Member turned against him. I consoled myself by the thought that I had made my position quite clear to them during the early autumn. I had closely consulted my chairman about the trend which events were then taking, and gained his approval for the ideas which I put forward. If I were now to support the Government, I could only do so by swallowing my words and what were already known to be my convictions. My constituents might accept my explanation. There was, however, a double danger: that they would feel that no matter what a Member had felt and said during the preliminary stages of the crisis, his place was unquestionably behind his leader now that discussion had been followed by action; and secondly that the circumstances since I made my speeches in September had been completely changed by the Israeli attack on Egypt. My fears were well-founded. They strongly held both views. I held neither.

This was no ordinary war. Half the population, not exclusively Socialists and Liberals, were opposed to it, and had given long notice what their attitude would be. In such circumstances the Government could not be surprised if some Conservatives in Parliament also expressed the views which a minority of Conservatives outside were known to hold. That was one of the foreseeable risks of the operation. An open expression of dissent was more excusable than at the outset of almost any other war in our recent history. It was to be so short a war that Conservative dissenters could easily remain silent until it was over. A protest at that stage would certainly do no further harm, and it might do some good. If I were an American, as shocked as his President by the Anglo-French ultimatum, and heard that a group of Conservatives had joined their protests to those of the official Opposition, my reaction would not have been to despise them as traitors, but to feel less resentful against England. I should have become more inclined to regard the incident as an aberration of policy instead of symptomatic of a whole new British attitude.

This was exactly what I believed myself. There had been nothing like the Suez action since the beginning of the century, and it is unlikely to be repeated. It seemed wholly inconsistent with the character of the Conservative party, and with the character of its present leaders. For a Conservative to dissociate himself from it, would not be a breach of party loyalty, but a reminder of one of the party's great principles, that we should conduct our foreign relations on the basis of respect for treaties and consultation with our allies and our Commonwealth. All of us had put forward this simple, even platitudinous, doctrine in our election speeches. The answer was given that the Suez crisis was wholly exceptional and justified a modification of this rule. I did not think so. It seemed to me an occasion when the rule should have been particularly observed. When it was not, a Member of Parliament who saw the situation in this light had a greater duty than his duty to obey his leader and his constituents. He would be serving his party best by opposing it.

Thus I reached my personal decision. I only knew for certain of a few other Conservatives in Parliament who felt in varying degrees as I did, although I have since heard of several more. We were still unorganized. Few of us knew of Anthony Nutting's or Sir Edward Boyle's impending resignations from the Government until they occurred, and neither of them attended our haphazard meetings. We met not more than twice as a group between the ultimatum and the cease-fire. We had never combined before and never combined afterwards. We let the Whips know of our attitude, but it remained in doubt until the last minute how many of us would actually abstain in the crucial vote of confidence on November 8th. In the event, eight of us did so. They were Sir Robert Boothby, Anthony Nutting, Sir Edward Boyle, J. J. Astor, Sir Frank Medlicott, Colonel Banks, William Yates, and myself. From none of us was the whip withdrawn. But within a month, one had resigned his seat in Parliament, one had become an Independent Member, one had previously announced his intention not to stand again, two had been ostracized by their constituency Associations, and two were in deep disgrace with theirs. Only Sir Robert Boothby emerged relatively unscathed.

When the division was called, I went to the library and read *The Illustrated London News*. Another Member, on his way to vote, paused to put his hand on the back of my chair. 'It looks to me,' he said, 'as if you are doing something which may be either very right or very wrong. But whichever it is, you need never feel ashamed of having done it.' I looked up to see who it was, but by that time he had hurried out between Pugin's brass-encrusted doors. I do not know if it was a Conservative or Labour Member. It could have been either.

Chapter Six

BOURNEMOUTH EAST
AND CHRISTCHURCH

Character of the constituency—Lord Quickswood, Major Grant and Sir Horace Wilson—earlier incidents—the Suez issue—I conceal my views till fighting has stopped—my UNA speech—Conservative reaction—my 'presumption and disloyalty'—vote of no-confidence against me on Dec. 5th 1956—should I have resigned?—Mr Macmillan's attitude to the dispute—adoption of Major Friend as prospective candidate—later developments in the controversy—the Young Conservatives—opinion of the Press and in Parliament—Major Friend promises unqualified support of party-line—am I a suitable Member for Bournemouth?—how the controversy can end

MY ABSTENTION from the vote of confidence on the Government's Suez policy led to the biggest political upheaval which Bournemouth has ever known. I will attempt to give a full and honest account of what happened: full, because if it is to be of any value as an illustration of the mechanism of constituency politics and the power of a local Conservative Association, it must not skimp essential facts; honest, because it would be doing a great injustice to my constituents to present a one-sided case, or to hold them up to ridicule for my own advantage.

I give this account as an example of what can occur when a Member and his constituency supporters disagree on a policy matter of the utmost gravity. I do not say that the Bournemouth incident is more important than several other controversies which took place at the same time and for much the same reasons, within the Labour constituency party at Wednesbury, for example, and in the Conservative Associations of Melton and Central Norfolk. I write about my own experience because I know most about it, and because it would be presumptuous for me to comment in detail upon the experiences of other Members about which I obviously cannot know all the facts.

The constituency of Bournemouth East and Christchurch, which I have represented in Parliament since February 1952, was created in 1948 by boundary changes which divided Bournemouth into two unequal halves. The larger half, Bournemouth

West, was allotted the centre of the town, together with the main hotels, shopping centres, and the wealthier suburbs; Bournemouth East included the big residential districts of Boscombe and Southbourne, to which was added, for parliamentary purposes, the neighbouring borough of Christchurch. It is an almost wholly urban constituency, 'one of the most agreeable,' as my predecessor, Brendan Bracken, wrote to me when he accepted a peerage in 1952, 'in the entire country.' Bournemouth has grown enormously in the last fifty years. It did not exist, even as a fishing village, until 1810, when Tregonwell built his mansion in 'an unreclaimed solitude' on a bluff overlooking the Bourne stream. Christchurch has a history extending back to the Bronze Age, and one of the most beautiful mediaeval churches in England. As early as 1307 it received its first recorded summons to send two burgesses to Parliament, and today it retains its individual character, in spite of its contiguity to its huge neighbour. It has been my frequent boast that I represent both the oldest and the youngest towns in Britain. It may not be quite true.

If you walk down Christchurch High Street, or along the quiet curving roads of Southbourne, you will realize at once that this constituency could never be anything else but Conservative. Except for a single Liberal lapse in 1906, it has always been so. Bournemouth has had among its recent Members of Parliament such great Conservative figures as Sir Henry Page-Croft, Sir Leonard Lyle and Brendan Bracken, and it was in Bournemouth that one of the very first Habitations of the Primrose League was founded in 1885. The Conservative majorities are enormous. My own increased from 14,000 in the by-election of 1952 to 18,500 in 1955.[1] This solid majority is made up of three types of people: the shop-keepers, proprietors of boarding-houses and small hotels, and the professional men; secondly, many of the workers in the two local aircraft factories and Ministry of Supply establishments; and thirdly, the retired, the widowed, and the single.

[1] The exact figures at the General Election of May 1955 were:

Nicolson, N. (Conservative)	28,757
Buckle, D. J. (Labour)	10,259
Molony, B. P. (Liberal)	4,851
Conservative majority	18,498

This last category is of particular importance in local Conservative life. The women provide a large part of the Association's membership of some five thousand, and do most of the work. The men, who in their retirement have come to live in Bournemouth, bring with them a combined experience ranging over the whole field of business, the Church, medicine, law, the civil and colonial services, and the armed forces. Most of them were only able to join a political party late in their lives, and they apply to it the same high standards of integrity and loyalty which became second nature to them throughout their professional careers.

I will mention three of them, the President of my Association, Lord Quickswood; the chairman, Major Grant; and one who subsequently gave me great support, Sir Horace Wilson.

Lord Quickswood, formerly Lord Hugh Cecil, lived in retirement in a large house at Boscombe. He was over 80. I had known him as a boy at Eton when he was Provost. 'Known' is an overstatement. I revered him. He once asked me to breakfast in the Provost's lodgings, and I was so nervous that my fish-cake leaped suddenly from my plate and rolled across the table into his lap. 'I'm glad,' he said, 'that I didn't do that first; but now I'm going to do it better,' and he bowled his own fish-cake like a Dutch cheese the whole length of the table. They were very hard fish-cakes. When next I met him, in 1952, as chairman of the Committee appointed to choose a candidate to succeed Brendan Bracken, I hoped that he wouldn't remember the fish-cake episode. If he did, he gave no sign of recognizing me, but with great courtesy and firmness, whipped the six rivals in and out of the parade-ring like a judge at a cattle-show. I looked forward, as Member, to a long association with this great man. But he was ill. Political discussion over-stimulated him. So although I quite often wrote to him, I only went occasionally to his house in Boscombe, and then I would steer the conversation on to safer subjects, such as oratory, of which he never tired of talking. ('Let your facts illustrate your arguments,' he once said to me. 'Never the other way round.' A priceless piece of advice.)

When I saw him, he was usually in bed, needlessly apologetic for his growing infirmities, and amused, I think, to see how the political accidents which had shaped his own career, were repeat-

5*

ing themselves in another generation. Independence of judgement was one of his constant themes; 'but it is an advantage,' he once added, with the laughter mounting inside him, 'if you can occasionally be right as well.' When I found myself in serious trouble in December 1956, he came at once to my aid with a stinging rebuke for the Association of which he was President: 'I have no hesitation whatever in saying that Mr Nicolson has done quite rightly in thus voting. He was sent to Parliament to be a representative of the whole Commons of the Realm speaking in the name of the whole Commons, and not as a delegate of the particular constituency who had the right to appoint him.'[1] It was the last letter he ever wrote. He died a week later. As I stood by his open grave at Hatfield, I knew that I had lost a valuable friend and ally.

The chairman of the Association, Major Grant, had a very different background. He had retired comparatively young after service in the Indian Army, and an ordeal as a prisoner-of-war in Japanese hands. His main interests in retirement were the Hampshire Red Cross and the Conservative Party. When I first knew him, he was chairman of the Highcliffe branch at the eastern extremity of the constituency, and at both my elections it had given me great pleasure to spend the last half hour of polling day in his company, so well had he organized his ward and so infectious was his enthusiasm. Until the moment of my disgrace we were on excellent terms. But after it, he felt that he could not allow a personal friendship to affect his judgement, and our mutual sympathy inevitably declined. He did what he honestly conceived to be his duty.

Sir Horace Wilson was not the leader of my supporters. That role belonged to one of my ex-chairmen, Brigadier J. S. Windsor, whose fervent encouragement buoyed me up throughout the controversy. Sir Horace was our elder statesman, and after Lord Quickswood's death, my most distinguished constituent. Even to my generation, his name was a legend. Head of the Civil Service, personal adviser to Neville Chamberlain, intermediary between Chamberlain and Hitler at the time of the Munich crisis, there is scarcely a man alive who has had a more intimate knowledge of

[1] For the text of the letter, see towards the end of the Appendix.

the relations between Civil Service, Cabinet and Parliament. He retired in 1942 into deliberate obscurity, and only emerged from it to take up the fight on my behalf, lending me his name and his presence on several of my platforms, from which he spoke in passionate advocacy of my cause. It cannot have been easy for him to do so. He was an elderly man. He had hitherto played no part in party politics. My own father had been among his strongest critics at the time of Munich. And those Conservatives who in 1938 had applauded Chamberlain, and had since forgotten how on his return from Munich he had given immediate orders for an intensification of our armament programme, now attributed to him and to his chief adjutant, Sir Horace Wilson, the blame, if any, which should be shared by the party as a whole. In spite of all this, and the obvious temptation to watch the battle from the side-lines, Sir Horace came unhesitatingly into the open, and his intervention had a great effect.

These were some of the main actors in the Bournemouth incident. Of myself, I need only say that I have never been a member of any political party other than the Conservative. I fought in its name two elections before I came to Bournemouth; at Leicester in 1950, and in the Falmouth and Camborne division of Cornwall in 1951. Though I lost both elections, I do not think that I disgraced myself at either. Both my previous chairmen, Mr W. B. Jarvis of Leicester and Captain Norman Black of Falmouth, were quick to send me messages of sympathy when I found myself in trouble at Bournemouth.

Before coming to the events of 1956, I must in fairness mention two other occasions when I offended my constituents. These incidents have lately been revived as proof that, apart from capital punishment and Suez, I was already regarded as a renegade.

Six weeks after my election, in March 1952, I made a speech at a luncheon of the Bournemouth Habitation of the Primrose League. According to the report in the local paper, this is what I said:

Too many Conservatives are indulging in a form of hatred against certain members of the other side—notably Mr Bevan. It is not in the tradition of the Conservative Party or the country. In our opinion Mr Bevan is misguided, but he is not wicked. If he became Prime Minister, there is no need for you to fear that he would eliminate whole categories or classes of the population, or plunge us into an alliance with Russia. You can only deal with people like that, not by hating them, but by understanding their point of view. If Conservatives go about saying, 'Bevan is a monster', they are only strengthening his hand.

There was a gasp of horror in the audience, for these were the days before Mr Bevan was considered respectable. I am not in the least proud of my speech. I think it was ill-expressed, tactless and jejune. Nevertheless, I do not think that what I said was untrue, or a sufficient basis on which to erect a theory that I am not really a Conservative at all, but a Socialist in disguise.

The second incident occurred about two years later. I was addressing a week-end conference of the Wessex Area Conservatives, and several of my own leading supporters were present. It was a private meeting confined to Conservatives, and my speech was not reported. The theme of it was that both main political parties desired precisely the same ends: they both wanted peace, and they both wanted prosperity: the only quarrel between them, and it was a serious quarrel, was about the means of attaining these ends. These observations sound trite, and they were. But they caused such consternation that I felt obliged to request a special meeting with the chief officers of my Association to justify my conduct. Fortunately, two representatives of Central Office had heard the speech, and in response to an appeal for their judgement, replied that they had found no fault with it; indeed, they had thought it quite stimulating.

I believe that these are the only two incidents of which complaint has been made. Their unorthodoxy is magnified in recollection. In between, stretched months and years of peace in the constituency. In 1953 I married, and bought a house near Christchurch. I felt welcome wherever I went. I enjoyed being the Member, and from what was said about me at successive Annual General Meetings, I felt my confidence growing and my position strengthening. At the time of the General Election of 1955, not a word that ever reached my ears was said publicly or privately against my readoption, and the election campaign itself created as close a bond between me and my supporters as any Member could desire. The demonstration at Christchurch Town Hall after the declaration of the poll went far beyond the cordiality normal on such occasions.

Then came capital punishment. I have described in a previous chapter that my attitude on this subject was well known in the constituency immediately before the election, when some protest could have been made, and none was; and how I modified it in response to Major Grant's personal appeal. I think it right that these facts should be remembered now. When it is said that I opposed my constituents' wishes, it might be added that when Parliament was about to make an irrevocable decision, I did what they wished me to do. Whether I was right or wrong to compromise, compromise I did, and I was the first of the Conservative abolitionists to promise complete support for Major Lloyd-George's Homicide Bill. 'Thinking people entirely agree with your action in that respect,' Major Grant wrote to me when the Suez quarrel was at its height, 'on the grounds that supporting a Private Member's Bill on a free vote is one thing, and opposing a Government Bill is something quite different.' I think that he is right. I only wish that he would occasionally remind the Association of this distinction, and of the action I took in response to his appeal.

This was the background of Suez: four years of peace, broken by two minor incidents; an election which was a triumph for the Association; capital punishment, on which I expressed disagreement with a majority of my electors and then compromised at the decisive stage in deference to their opinions; an autumn series of constituency speeches against the use of force to solve the Canal problem; and then catastrophe.

A meeting between myself and the Executive Council to discuss the Middle East had already been planned for late November, but the ultimatum forestalled it. Within twenty-four hours of hearing the Prime Minister's statement in the House, I telephoned to Major Grant, and told him that I could not support the Government for the reasons, among others, which I had explained in my autumn speeches. Though he much regretted my decision, he agreed with me that it would be right to say nothing until the fighting in the Canal Zone was over. I had to make two constituency speeches that week-end. It would be impossible to avoid

the topic which was in everybody's mind. I therefore suggested
that I should state the Government's case for intervention, without stating my objections to it. Major Grant agreed that this was
the best course.

I have never had to make two more difficult speeches. My
audiences were bewildered by the ultimatum, and I had to explain
it. As I carried on, 'The Prime Minister says . . .', 'The Government feel . . .', I could sense the atmosphere lightening. I was convincing them by the arguments which I would later have to
destroy, and strengthening the attack on myself which I foresaw
must follow. 'Not many knew, as I knew,' Major Grant gallantly
said at a later stage, 'that in his first two speeches, Mr Nicolson
was loyally trying to present the Government's view objectively,
suppressing his own objections and misgivings for the moment
because our troops were then about to go into action.' At the
second meeting, I had to contend with one or two Conservatives
in the audience who strongly criticized the Government's action,
and reminded me of my own autumn speeches. I could only reply,
'The Prime Minister would probably answer your question by
saying . . .' Though I said nothing to commit myself, I realized
that few people who heard me could have imagined that I agreed
with the questioner and not with the Prime Minister. I let only
one hint drop of my real feelings, when I said, 'the truest loyalty
consists in conviction after self-examination,' and afterwards I
told the critics privately that I shared their views, explaining why
I did not yet feel able to say so publicly. I gave the same warning
to several of the Association's branch-chairmen, and I was careful
to see that my name was not attached to any telegram of unqualified support sent to Downing Street. It was an unpleasant
task, convinced though I was that it was necessary. If I had spoken
out at once, my crime would have been doubled. It would have
been said, with some justification, that I had stabbed the troops in
the back. A charge of inconsistency, though undeserved, was
preferable to that.

These two speeches were made on November 2nd and 3rd,
1956. On Sunday the 4th, I went to see Major Grant in his house,
and handed him a letter explaining why I could not support the
Government. I asked him to show it in confidence to any of the

leading officers of the Association, but not for the moment to give it wider circulation. I returned home to listen to Mr Gaitskell's broadcast on television, and heard him appeal to Conservative back-bench Members to desert their leader. I was horrified. I realized that of the ten or twelve million people to whom he was then speaking, I was one of the handful to whom he was addressing his main message. I knew that it would be said (as it was said) that I had responded to his appeal, although I had made my firm decision several days before, and had given formal notice of it to my chairman a few hours earlier. It was the only moment when I felt tempted to withdraw.

On November 6th the Prime Minister announced the cease-fire, and our acceptance of the United National Emergency Force. On the 8th there was to be a full debate in the House of Commons, followed by a vote of confidence in the Government. I knew that I must abstain, but I did not wish to do so without first explaining my reasons. The chance of catching the Speaker's eye in the debate was, I knew, slender. Therefore, when the secretary of the United Nations Association rang me up in London on the morning of the 7th to ask if I knew of anyone who would be free to speak to the Bournemouth UNA Branch that evening, I seized the opportunity. I said I would go myself. It was exactly the platform I needed at the very moment when I needed it. My speech would be made in a hall within a mile of my own constituency boundary, in the centre of Bournemouth, where many of my constituents could attend. It would be made to an all-party organization of which Sir Anthony himself was President, and which stood for the international principles to which my own party had so frequently pledged itself. I immediately telephoned my intentions to the Association's agent, Arthur Cowley. I told him that my speech that night would lead to great controversy, and might even split the Association. 'If there is any doubt in your mind,' I added, 'about your own position, let me make it clear that your duty is not to me, but to your Executive Council.' I knew that it would be a heavy blow to him, as he was a deeply loyal Conservative, and he and I had worked amicably together for so long. Never then, or at any later stage, did he say or do anything to alter my opinion of his integrity, and I am grateful to him for it.

Mr Cowley met me at the hall when I arrived, and handed me a letter of bitter reproach from Major Grant.

'I think and feel at least as strongly in support of the Prime Minister as you appear to be against him,' he wrote. 'I know that the vast majority of people who worked so hard for you, and of the 28,000 who voted for you, giving you one of the biggest majorities in the country, look to you to support the Government and not to join the Socialists in attacking him. . . . We would be ashamed and humiliated if the Member we elected so proudly only eighteen months ago should now add his voice to those raucous voices opposite, who have only their miserable party advantage in mind. . . . I am deeply disappointed in you. When the plaudits of the UNA crowd are sounding in your ears tonight, I hope that you will remember that thousands will look upon your action as a betrayal of those who trusted you to support the cause in which their deepest feelings are engaged.

I only had time to glance at the letter before I mounted the platform, but even in those few anxious minutes, I could not help respecting an intensity of feeling which matched my own.

I made the speech. It was the first public back-bench protest against the Suez policy. 'A Government should never put the country in a position where it can be condemned by the rest of the world of duplicity and aggression,' I said. 'A Member of Parliament must oppose his own party when he feels that the pledges he has given his electors in its name have been broken. I will not withdraw what I have said under any circumstances—I repeat, under any circumstances whatever.' A Brigadier rose to his feet and walked out of the hall. Several speakers of all parties came forward from the audience and condemned or praised what they had heard. I had almost no Conservative support. I returned home, and waited for the storm to burst next day.

When it came, it took two forms. There was the charge of disloyalty, which was the most persistent; and the charge of presumption, that I should dare to set myself up as a greater authority on international relations than the Prime Minister. The latter charge was the more difficult to deal with. Of course there was no statesman in the country, and probably none in the whole world, who had more knowledge of international affairs than Sir Anthony Eden. Against that I could only put my meagre experience as a

British delegate to the Council of Europe, and my recent travels in the Middle East and America. Even though I had studied the problem as deeply as I have ever studied any, and had been broadcasting fortnightly to the Middle East on the BBC's overseas service for the last two years, it would be absurd to claim that I had half the knowledge or experience of any member of the Cabinet. But this was a matter on which every person, whether a Minister, a Member, or one of his constituents, had a duty to make up his own mind. The essential facts were known to all. The principles involved were self-evident. There was only one question: if the means which we employed at Port Said were such as to antagonize almost the whole world, should we have embarked on the operation at all? Everybody could now see the results of it. The crisis was already in its post-mortem stage. If our action had been wise, why had it not also been successful?

Because, the answer came, people like myself had betrayed the Prime Minister. I pointed out that I had remained quiet until the operation had already failed; and that the phrase 'people like myself' included most of the population of the world, and half the population of our own country. But it was true that the vast majority of the Conservative Party had supported the Prime Minister, and that in subsequent by-elections the Conservative vote dropped only fractionally. I was almost alone in being out of step. 'If the average Conservative,' wrote one of my correspondents, 'can silence any doubts out of loyalty to the party and faith in the Prime Minister, surely a Member of Parliament can do the same?' My chairman wrote, after referring to my autumn speeches, 'when action started, an entirely new situation arose: the die was cast, unity and loyalty were the only things that mattered, and we looked to you for them in vain. What you did, in addition to being disloyal, seems to me presumptuous, self-opinionated, mean and unworthy.' I replied that I had never protested that my Association were being disloyal to their Member (though in a sense they were), because I recognized that they were faced by a conflict of loyalties. So was I, but it was a different conflict. I was looking beyond the Prime Minister to the reputation of our party and country; they were looking beyond me to the ordeal through which Sir Anthony was passing. They

regarded his illness as an additional reason for giving him unqualified support; I regarded it as a reason why, on this single
occasion, his judgement might have erred. I thought, like Burke:

There are men, who out of love to their country and their kind, would
torture their invention to find excuses for the mistakes of their brethren;
and who to stifle dissension, would construe doubtful appearances with
the utmost favour.[1]

That I appeared to be siding with the Socialists against my own
party made my behaviour doubly inexcusable. Yet the fact that
the Labour Party had consistently opposed a policy of force, was
among my main motives for opposing it myself. I believed that a
nation like our own should only resort to an act of large-scale
violence when opinion in favour of it is almost unanimous. 'It
should never be forgotten,' Sir Frank Medlicott had written to
the Prime Minister when he took the same decision as myself,
'that in the two great wars, the margin between victory and defeat
was perilously narrow, and in my view the margin by which we
triumphed was due solely to the nation-wide conviction that we
were in the right.' I wholly endorsed his words. A Government
can use its majority in the House of Commons to do anything it
wishes against the will of the Opposition, except one thing: it
should not go to war.

During the month which followed the UNA meeting, I made
no public attempt to justify my conduct, except by a single letter
to the local paper. I was told that a special meeting of the whole
Association had been called for December 5th, at which I would
have an opportunity to state my case. Meanwhile the Executive
Council had met to repudiate my views and pledge their loyalty to
the Government. They also drew up a resolution to be debated at
the special meeting. It deplored my speech of November 7th on
the grounds that it had 'caused embarrassment to the Prime
Minister and Government, misrepresented the views of the vast
majority of his supporters in the constituency, and encouraged
and delighted the Opposition.' There was an ominous item to be
considered at the close of the debate on this resolution:

[1] Speech previous to the election of 1780.

4. Instruct the Executive Council to take such action as may be deemed necessary.

The meeting at the Selwyn Hall, Boscombe, on December 5th, 1956, was the only occasion, before or since, that I have been given an opportunity to speak to my Association, or any part of it, in my defence. I was refused permission to attend the Executive Council when my conduct was discussed. I was not allowed to visit any of the branch committees when they were framing their own resolutions for submission to the special meeting. I was in quarantine. Thus, when the date of the meeting came, the inner core of the Association had not only reached a verdict, but in their minds had passed sentence, before the accused had been heard at all. My speech was not even a speech from the dock: it was a speech from the condemned cell. It was delivered to an audience of 400 people out of the 8,000 members of the Association, the 28,000 who had voted for me at the previous election, and the 60,000 who composed my total electorate. My fate lay in the hands of less than one per cent of those to whom I was ultimately responsible.

I do not blame the organizers. They had booked the largest hall in the constituency, and it was only to be expected that the most ardent party-workers would come early, some on foot, others in organized coach-loads from the more distant part of the constituency, to fill the few available seats. When I arrived at 7.30 p.m. the police were doing their best to quieten an angry crowd against whom the doors had been shut. As I fought my way through to the side-door, there were cries of 'We're all with you, but we can't get in!' and 'The meeting's been packed', mingled with some boos and other indications that they were by no means all on my side. I made them a short speech, as the thin rain fell. 'Look,' I said, 'there's an angry crowd outside, and an even angrier one inside. I can't face you both simultaneously. I'm sorry you can't all get in, but to blame me would be like blaming the lamb for the arrangements in the slaughterhouse. I expect that those inside are as good a cross-section of the constituency as those outside, and when this business is over, we'll hold other meetings in other parts of the constituency to which you can all come.' I then went into the back-room of the hall, where I found the chief officers of the Association and the area agent looking remarkably grim.

The area agent suggested that the whole meeting should be postponed till a later date, when we could hold it in the much larger Town Hall in central Bournemouth. I disagreed. I said that I had been given special leave to miss an important debate in the House, and that not only did I wish to say what I had come to say, but the audience would never allow us to send them away empty-handed. Major Grant then asked me if I would accept the verdict of the meeting as valid. I replied: 'They must do what they think fit, and I will do what I think fit. But if they ask me to resign the seat, I shall refuse.' There was much discussion about those words at a later stage of the controversy. Some thought that I had implicitly agreed to abide by the decision of the meeting, short of resignation. I consider that my words meant no more than that we were all entitled to state our points of view, but I would not hold myself bound by any resolution that might be passed. Whether my meaning was clear or not, that is certainly what I had intended. I regret the ambiguity. The circumstances did not favour precision.

We climbed the short flight of steps to the platform. There was an immediate outburst of booing, and a few cheers. The proceedings opened with a speech by Major Grant, in which he fairly summarized the course of the dispute until that date. The chairmen or secretaries of the twelve branches then came in turn to the foot of the platform, and read out the resolutions which their committees had passed without consulting the main body of their members. The resolutions were all hostile. Eight of them called for my immediate resignation. Finding it difficult to know whether to smile, appear indifferent, or look remorseful, while this quarter-hour's indictment continued, I pulled a sheet of paper towards me and took a careful note of each resolution as it was read out. I have it still. The same words and phrases recur: 'forfeited confidence', 'emphatically deplores', 'untold harm', 'disloyal', 'resign'. It was every politician's nightmare come true.

I then spoke for about forty minutes.[1] I ended with the words: 'It is for those reasons, with which I believe you will one day all

[1] The speech is reproduced in the Appendix.

agree, even if some of you do not agree now, that I must decline any invitation to resign my seat.' The speech was heard in almost complete silence. Only when I said, 'we should have informed the Americans and the Commonwealth, who would have helped us . . .', was there a stir of incredulity. When I quoted Churchill's magnificent words about parliamentary democracy, I thought for a fleeting moment that I might have the majority with me. But when my wife and I were asked to leave the hall at the end of my speech, I knew that I had lost. Dr E. W. Deane, another previous chairman of the Association, whose support for me never wavered, followed us home an hour later to tell us what had happened in our absence.

A local Conservative Councillor mounted the platform and said: 'You have listened to a long and skilful torrent of words. Your attention has been diverted from the issue. Are you going to be represented by a loyal Conservative or not? Do you want Nicolson or Eden? (Cries of 'Eden! Eden!') Whom do you want, a Conservative or a piebald politician?'[1] He was followed by another speaker who reminded the audience of my 'Socialistic utterances' at the Primrose League, and of a book which my firm had published about Guy Burgess. But it was not all one-sided. Several speakers, including Brigadier Windsor, pleaded for moderation. But clearly the branch resolutions which had been drawn up many days previously, and were read out before I made my speech, had already committed a large part of the audience to vote against me.

A motion was finally put to the meeting in these terms:

'This meeting regrets that it has no further confidence in the intention of Mr Nigel Nicolson adequately to represent in Parliament the political views of Bournemouth East and Christchurch Conservatives, and instructs the Executive Council to take steps to obtain a prospective Conservative Candidate to contest the constituency at the next Parliamentary Election.'

It was carried by 298 votes to 92. I was surprised that the minority vote was so large.

[1] This quotation is taken from the report in the *Bournemouth Daily Echo*, December 6th, 1956.

I had naturally considered whether I should resign the seat. The Chairman of the party, Mr Oliver Poole, encouraged me not to do so, and no demand for my resignation was ever made to me officially by Major Grant. But I feared at one moment that to insist on my constitutional rights and remain on as Member after a vote of no-confidence had been passed on me, would put me in the position of a sacked housemaid who insists on her week's notice. In much the same circumstances, Stanley Evans, the Labour Member for Wednesbury, who had supported the Suez policy, acceded to his constituency party's demand for his resignation, explaining that 'a general without an army, living on borrowed time, seldom wields much influence, and loses all dignity.' Anthony Nutting had taken the same decision to resign his seat at Melton, 'to avoid a deep split in his Association,' and because his Executive had sent a telegram of support to Downing Street before he had had a chance to explain his attitude to them. *The Times* had commented on the Wednesbury case that the attitude of the constituency party 'deserves nothing but censure. Mr Evans is free to act as his conscience bids him, but he should not expect his action to be regarded, now or ever, as an example.'[1] This seemed to be the general view of Parliament. I was strongly pressed by fellow-Members not to resign. A principle of some importance was at stake. If a series of resignations followed constituency pressure over Suez, no Members except the most servile could consider themselves safe in future. Simultaneously, I received a great many letters from Bournemouth Conservatives, begging me to stand firm, and a small group, headed by Brigadier Windsor, was soon formed to support me. Only one person put forward the idea that I should resign and stand at the ensuing by-election as an Independent. It was not a good idea. It would have put the constituency to the expense and trouble of an election campaign which they did not want, and split the Conservative vote. For these many reasons, I decided to remain, and carry on with my parliamentary duties as if nothing had happened. I hoped that in time passions might cool, and that among the 28,000 local Conservatives who had not been at the Selwyn Hall, there might be many who would come forward to help me.

[1] *The Times*. November 27th, 1956.

The resolution passed at the meeting on December 5th did not call for an immediate selection of a new prospective candidate, and I soon suggested to Major Grant that its implementation should be delayed to give time for Conservatives to reflect, and to enable me to go round the branches and discuss with them what had happened. I told him that I did not dispute that an Association has the constitutional right to disown or expel its Member: I only questioned whether it was a happy precedent to have done so in the heat of the moment, and because of my disagreement on a single point of policy, on the merits of which there were widespread doubts throughout the country. Only a very small proportion of the Association had taken part in the decision. Lord Quickswood, the President of the Association, and two of its ex-chairmen, had supported me. There had been an outcry in the national press. Several Conservative Members had written letters of protest to the newspapers pointing out the sorry implications of the Bournemouth incident. Many local Conservatives were deeply disturbed. Would it not be better, in the party's interests, before going to the full length of breaking all connection with me, to pause a while? I suggested that we should resume normal relations, on the understanding that I was on trial. I promised to accept as final the verdict of the Association two years ahead, or as soon as an election appeared imminent, whichever was the sooner. Meanwhile I would do my utmost in both my parliamentary and constituency work to prove that Bournemouth East had a Member of whom they had no reason to feel ashamed. If, on the other hand, a prospective candidate were to be adopted immediately, the Association would be irretrievably split.

Major Grant rejected these arguments. The Association was already split, he said. I had split it. Only a new man could restore unity. It was presumptuous of me to suggest that I should be permitted to go round the branches, 'to renew your attacks on the Eden Government.' The breach was complete. Henceforward no branch would be permitted to invite me to address them; my annual donation to the Association's funds was returned; I could not use the office even to interview constituents; and the allegiance of the whole Association would be transferred from me to the new candidate as soon as he was selected. A selection committee was set up on December 17th, and they soon had some sixty names in front of them.

The attitude of Conservative Central Office and the party leaders was one of non-intervention. Their public comments on the affair were generalized and carefully guarded. But it was clear that the behaviour of my Association contrasted strongly with the party's tradition of tolerance, which at this time was frequently reaffirmed. For instance, Mr Harold Macmillan, in his speech on accepting the leadership of the party on January 22nd, 1957, said: 'We do not believe in expelling people. I think that is a good thing, because I, no doubt, would have been a candidate for expulsion many years ago. It is this tolerance which makes us a national party.' A few days earlier, he had underlined his words by admitting to his new Government both Sir Edward Boyle and Mr Julian Amery; the first had resigned from the Eden Government in protest against the Suez action, and the second had been a leader of the group which strongly opposed our withdrawal. Sir Edward Boyle, on taking up his new office at the Ministry of Education, had been permitted to comment, 'I do not unsay one word of what I have said on Suez.' But neither Mr Oliver Poole, the Chairman of the party, nor Mr Macmillan, thought it right to give my Association any public advice, and Lord Hailsham, when he succeeded to the Chairmanship, took the same view. A constituency Association was autonomous. Unless it breaks one of the party's rules, the party leadership cannot interfere. Mine had broken no rule. It had acted within its undoubted rights, and it had been guided throughout by the area agent, whose role was to see that nothing unconstitutional was done.

Eventually, on February 11th, 1957, Major Grant wrote to the Prime Minister at my suggestion and with the consent of Mr Poole, asking for his views on the matter, and informing him that the Executive were selecting a candidate that very night. This was Mr Macmillan's reply, which was published in the local paper a few days later:

February 12th 1957   10 Downing Street
Dear Major Grant,
    The Chairman of the Party organization has kept me informed of the situation which has developed between the Bournemouth East and

Christchurch Conservative Association and the Member of Parliament for the Division, Mr Nigel Nicolson. It is a very long tradition of our Party that the Leader of the Party should not intervene in matters between a Member and his constituents. I am sure the Association in deciding its action will bear in mind the best interests of the Conservative Party, nationally as well as locally.

I am sending a copy of this letter to Mr Nigel Nicolson, and would have no objection to your publishing your letter and my reply in the Press if you wish to do so.

Signed: Harold Macmillan

I was left to make the most I could of the phrase 'the best interests of the Conservative Party, nationally as well as locally.' But it was too late. Major James Friend had been selected and proclaimed as the prospective candidate two days before the Prime Minister's letter was even received.

Major Friend was a stranger to Bournemouth, as I had been when I was adopted in 1952. He came from Staffordshire, where he managed his step-son's agricultural estates. His background was Harrow, Sandhurst, and the 11th Hussars, in which he received a regular commission in 1936. He served three years in Palestine, and had a gallant war record. He was three times mentioned in dispatches. He fought with his regiment in Africa and Normandy, and commanded the Second Army Forward Press Unit in Germany and Denmark. After the war he twice contested Newcastle-under-Lyme unsuccessfully as the Conservative candidate, but on both occasions he increased the minority vote.

He immediately impressed his personality on the constituency. At a press-conference on February 11th, he made the following comments. On his previous political experience at Newcastle: 'I believe my increased poll was chiefly due to local leadership which I learned as a regimental officer in the hills of Palestine and in the desert.' On Bournemouth: 'I am terribly proud to follow in the footsteps of many distinguished men, but in particular Henry Page-Croft, who championed the cause of the Empire.' On colonial and foreign policy: 'We must have the moral fibre here at home to maintain law and order in our possessions, without which we face extinction by younger nations.' On Suez: 'I greatly regret that we did not occupy all the Canal, though I am humble enough to understand that living as a farmer in Staffordshire, I have no access to Foreign Office information or Cabinet secrets.' On Sir Edward Boyle: 'As he is obviously very young and in-experienced, they are giving him a second chance.' On myself: 'I would rather not bring Mr Nicolson in; it makes it very difficult. I had never heard of him until the Hanging Bill, when he agreed with Mr Silverman.'[1]

All political parties have room for many different types, and clearly Major Friend and I are very different types of Conservative. I believe in negotiating on more equal terms with people who would once have accepted our orders without question, such as Asiatic dictators, colonial peoples or British Trades Union leaders. Major Friend thinks that this is a sign of weakness. I believe that we are still a great country, but great in a different way, and that our future role lies in putting our diplomatic skill, our scientific inventiveness and commercial genius at the disposal of the whole world. Major Friend and Conservatives like him think that we can continue to be great in the old way. I consider that by this approach they are not only exposing themselves to countless disappointments, but missing countless opportunities, and that it is not along those lines that Mr Macmillan is leading us. So, with Major Friend's arrival, a new factor subtly entered the Bournemouth controversy. My constituents were being asked to choose between two men; but they were now also asked to choose between two attitudes. Both of us were genuine Conservatives, but I was glad that the Association had not chosen a candidate politically almost indistinguishable from myself.

Major Friend bought a house at Christchurch as soon as he was officially adopted by the Association as their prospective candidate, and spends much of his time addressing the branch-meetings from which I am barred. He is my shadow-Member. I carry out all the normal constituency engagements; he makes himself agreeable to my constituents. It may seem an impossible relationship for both of us, but it is truer to say that there is no relationship at all. We never appear on the same occasions; we never refer to each other except obliquely in our speeches; and he has been most scrupulous in avoiding any public comment on the

[1] *Bournemouth Daily Echo*. February 12th, 1957.

dispute. His position is no more equivocal than mine. I am the elected Member; he is the official prospective candidate. At the time of writing (June 1958) we have never met. On one occasion only have we corresponded. I wrote to him on April 1st, 1957, explaining my future plans, and ended my long letter, 'I thought you would personally like to know what I am thinking and intending, rather than to allow rumour to embitter our relationship. My motives have always been open and honourable, and I know the same to be true of yourself.' His reply was so short that I can give it in full:

6th April 1957   Charnes Hall,
                                        Eccleshall, Staffordshire.
Dear Mr Nicolson,
    I have read the letter which you sent to me from the House of Commons on April Fool's Day.
                          Yours sincerely,
                          James Friend.

Basically, the situation has not changed since that date. Major Friend was officially adopted as prospective candidate at a meeting of the Association on March 6th, 1957, when he received 569 votes to 176. At the Annual General Meeting of the Association three weeks later, a vote of confidence in Major Grant and the Executive was carried by 495 to 46. That was the lowest point in my fortunes. I had not yet mobilized my strength. I held four public meetings in different parts of the division in February and March, at which I was supported by such men as Sir Frank Markham, MP, Lord Glyn and Sir Horace Wilson. At the first of these meetings, in Southbourne, the audience had voted in my favour by a majority of 274 to 73, but as it was unofficial, this vote could not be held to reverse the previous vote of no-confidence. The Southbourne Branch of the Association was closed to all new applicants for membership. I felt certain that if I were allowed to address the branches of the Association, and could persuade my Conservative supporters who were not already members of the Association to join it as soon as they were allowed to, I would eventually achieve a majority.

It was on these two points that the controversy flared up again

at intervals during the autumn of 1957 and the winter of 1958.
I contended that the vote at the Selwyn Hall had been a vote to
approve a certain immediate action, the selection of a prospective
candidate. It was not a vote which could commit the Association
to adopt Major Friend as the official candidate at the election two
or three years ahead. If the Association became dissatisfied with
him, or came to consider that I had been treated too harshly, they
must have every opportunity to reverse their previous decision. I
wrote to Major Grant in November 1957:

A constituency Association has every right to change its Member of
Parliament. . . . They may decide, when the next election comes, that
they would prefer another candidate in place of myself. With that
decision I would have no quarrel. . . . But in the interval majority
opinion may have changed. Some may have second thoughts on Suez;
others may find their support for Major Friend wavering, for he too
is on trial. The very membership of the Association will be different
in 1959 than it was in 1956. Some Conservatives will have died, others
resigned, others left the district, and newcomers will have joined.
Surely, then, it would be unreasonable, as well as unconstitutional, to
treat the candidature as a foregone conclusion?

   If it were made impossible for members of the Association, old
or new, to reverse the 1956 decision, by insisting on a pledge of
support to Major Friend as a condition of membership, then I
would obviously be unable to regain any lost ground. I would
have no choice but to set up my own Association, and to stand
as an Independent Conservative candidate at the election, so that
I could submit the issue to the electorate as a whole. I did not
wish to do this. I had given a promise that I would not. I had said
that I was willing to accept the final verdict of local Conservatives
immediately before the election, if it could be freely and fairly
given. It was therefore with alarm that I heard that a branch of
the Young Conservatives was threatened with disbandment because they had invited me to address them; and, later, that a new
enrolment form had been introduced, requiring some applicants
for membership to sign a pledge that they would on no account
support me against Major Friend.
   Many of the Young Conservatives had been among my sym-
pathizers from the start. Two of their chief officers, Leonard Allen

and John Little, had resigned from the Executive in January when my peace offer was rejected, and the strongest Young Conservative branch in the Association, the Boscombe East branch, defied the ban on inviting me to address them. I went to them twice, once in January and again in June 1957, and Major Friend also addressed them on other occasions. Of the two rivals, I undoubtedly had the friendlier reception. But the branch were not committed to support me against him. They declared that they wished to meet us both periodically, so that they could make up their minds between us. It was a reasonable request, but it stirred the Executive to angry action. The Young Conservatives were told by the agent, Mr Cowley, that if they held the second meeting, the Executive could disband the branch. So they skilfully converted it into 'a meeting for young people', and held it outside the official auspices of the Association. In September, they announced that they would send the profit from their jumblesale to the Conservative Central Office, instead of to the Association's headquarters. The Executive then issued their ultimatum. If the Boscombe East Young Conservatives did not come to heel within two weeks, the branch would be suspended. They refused. They decided unanimously against giving the required assurance that they would support Major Friend exclusively, and on October 28th they were formally suspended. They reconstituted themselves immediately as the Boscombe East Independent Young Conservatives, and gained increasingly in strength.

This incident fanned the embers of the dispute into a new blaze. Very soon afterwards the Executive took steps to see that such insubordination would not be repeated. A special enrolment form was devised for those who, like the Young Conservatives, would not accept the decision of December 1956 as final. They were required to 'abide by all resolutions of the Executive Council and General Meetings of the Association', and those who refused to sign, were told that they were ineligible for membership. The form was defended on the grounds that every democratic body requires a similar undertaking from its members to abide by majority decisions. But in that case, it was asked, how could the Selwyn Hall decision be reversed even if a majority wished to reverse it? If they gave the pledge demanded of them, they would be prevented from even raising the issue of the candidature. The Association would be committed to Major Friend, whether it wanted him or not, and it would come to consist of branches under threat of expulsion, and of individuals who had signed away their right to disagree. 'Is that the banner,' asked the *Christchurch Times*, 'under which the local Conservative vote is to be mustered at the next Election?'

Feeling therefore ran high again in the first two months of 1958. Many people who had hitherto supported the Executive, thought that the enrolment form was a constitutional outrage. The Executive were in danger of suffering their first defeat. At the Annual General Meeting in March they withdrew the form, and membership is now once more open to all *bone fide* Conservatives, whether they support me or Major Friend.

Such is the history of the Bournemouth affair up till the summer of 1958. The action of my Executive Council had the opposite effect from that which they intended. It did not unite local Conservatives; it divided them still further. It did not please the national leaders of the party; it caused them considerable embarrassment.

If I were to succeed in regaining the majority support of my Association, and became once again the official Conservative candidate at the next General Election, I believe that the party would be thankful. I do not say this because I regard myself as a particular asset to the Conservative Party, but because the Bournemouth incident has naturally been quoted to the party's discredit (notably by several Liberal spokesmen at the Torrington by-election in the spring of 1958) as an example of its monolithic crushing power. It would undoubtedly be quoted again at the next General Election, particularly by Liberals, unless in the interval I had succeeded in reversing the decision of December 1956. Is it not quite obvious that the Liberal and Labour candidates in Bournemouth East must be hoping for my defeat? It would give them an important hold on the floating vote. They would identify the whole party with the intolerance of a few, and attribute to all Conservatives the political opinions of Major Friend. Unfair though this charge would be, it would nevertheless be made. Thus, even for purely tactical reasons, there are good grounds for local Conservatives to reconsider their past decisions.

There is an even more important reason. Opinion outside Bournemouth East almost unanimously regarded my excommunication as having set an unfortunate political precedent. Over all these twenty months I have only read a single press comment, in the Cross-bencher column of the *Sunday Express* on March 17th, 1957, which commended the Executive's attitude. All the others, from *The Times* to the *Daily Mirror*, the *Daily Telegraph* to the *Spectator*, condemned it. *The Times* put the central question in a leading article entitled *An Oppressive Party Caucus*: 'The issue of public importance in this dispute is whether a member of Parliament is to be free without reprisals to adopt an attitude which clashes with that of the stalwarts who run the party machine in his constituency.'[1] The *Economist* asked:

Do the public in general, and Members of Parliament in particular, honestly believe that Members' conduct would be wiser or more in the public interest, if directed more closely by local committees?[2]

The *Daily Telegraph* said in its Peterborough column: 'I hope that Bournemouth Conservatives will be left in no doubt of the harm being done to the reputation of the whole party.'[3] Other comments have been to the same effect.

If this was solely the opinion of leader-writers and columnists, Bournemouth Conservatives might reply that it need have no influence on their judgement. But it is also the opinion of a great majority of the Conservative parliamentary party. There have been some Members like Brigadier Terence Clarke, the Member for Portsmouth West, and Colonel Bromley-Davenport, the Member for Knutsford, who have spoken on Major Friend's behalf. But there have been many others who have firmly, even harshly, declined every invitation from my Association, and have offered me their help instead. At first, I was reluctant to involve the parliamentary party in my dispute, and apart from Sir Frank

[1] *The Times.* March 21st, 1958.
[2] *Economist.* January 12th, 1957.
[3] *Daily Telegraph.* March 17th, 1958.

Markham's visit in its early days, I have only done so once. On March 21st, 1958, four Conservative Members, Maurice Macmillan, John Peyton, Sir Hugh Lucas-Tooth and Miss Joan Vickers, appeared on a Bournemouth platform under my chairmanship, and the Financial Secretary to the Treasury, Mr J. E. S. Simon, who at the last minute was unable to join them as arranged, sent a friendly message to be read out at the meeting. This demonstration had considerable effect. It would be simple for me to repeat it by bringing down to Bournemouth similar teams. But I cannot believe that my Association would wish to convert Bournemouth into a parliamentary battlefield. They have already had proof enough of the feeling at Westminster, and I am sure that they will give it the weight which it deserves. Our dispute cannot be considered in isolation. By a strange accident, we have jointly become involved in a situation which raises a political principle of much more than local importance. It would be wrong, in my opinion, if the views of the world outside were to be disregarded by those local Conservatives who alone have the power to decide.

They should also consider the very difficult position in which Major Friend would be placed if he were to become the official candidate at the General Election, and later the Member. He would be the symbol of an attitude which was almost universally deplored. During the election campaign his name would be a synonym for intolerance, and on reaching Westminster it would take him years to live down the circumstances of his election. No doubt he is well able to stand disapproval without flinching, but it will make it all the more difficult for him to do credit to his constituency, if the constituency had not done credit to his party.

That is the least of his troubles. Much more serious is the problem which he will face when, like myself, he finds himself in disagreement with the party, locally or nationally. He has already given one indication of his attitude to this problem, and it fills me with alarm. At his adoption meeting on March 6th, 1957, he said that the relationship of a candidate to his Association should be one 'of equal partnership cemented by mutual confidence'. Nobody could dispute that this is a good general definition, but it begs the important question. It was immediately put to him very bluntly:

He was asked whether, if elected, he would support the Government on any major issue whatever and accept the guidance of the Association whatever strong personal convictions he might have to the contrary. He replied that so long as the Government was a Conservative Government he would support it.[1]

According to another press report of the same answer, he added: 'An MP should do as his party wants on major issues of policy.'[2] That was a very terrible undertaking. But it was difficult for him to give any other, since the only reason why he was asked the question was to give him the opportunity to distinguish sharply between his attitude to dissent and mine. He could not mount a platform in my place and declare that he intended to repeat the same crime for which I had just been thrown off it.

Let us imagine that Major Friend had sat in the House of Commons during the Suez crisis. He would have strongly supported the ultimatum to Egypt, but he would have regretted, as he has told us, the failure 'to occupy all the Canal'. When the moment came in May to vote on the Government's decision to allow British ships to use the Canal, he would have been tempted to join the fifteen Conservatives who abstained, among whom was John Eden, the Member for Bournemouth West. But having given an unqualified pledge to 'do as his party wants on major issues of policy', he would have been bound to vote in defiance of his strongest convictions. Again, if an occasion arose when his Association wished him to vote in one way, and his Whips in a different way, he would be obliged either to break his pledge, or to offend his most important constituents. His position would become intolerable, his reputation in the House of Commons already compromised. No Member or prospective candidate should ever be asked for such a pledge, or ever give it. If Members are used as rubber-stamps, they will behave like rubber-stamps, and the whole purpose of Parliament will be defeated.

There remain two questions. Am I a proper person to represent

---

[1] *The Times*. March 7th, 1957.
[2] *The Bournemouth Times*. March 8th, 1957.

a constituency like Bournemouth East? And how is this controversy to end?

The soundest argument for replacing me by Major Friend is that he is more suited to the constituency than I am. It has been said that I stand for a type of Conservatism which is not the Conservatism of a majority of my local party-members, and that if I do not go now, there will be other occasions when I will find myself at odds with the Association, and the whole unhappy situation will arise again. I realize the force of that argument, and this is my answer to it.

I believe without reservation in all the basic principles of Conservatism. I am proud to belong to the party. I have never belonged to any other. I joined it after the war, when Mr Butler was in the process of transforming it. Once again it is slowly adapting itself to new conditions, with a flexibility that is the envy of its opponents. How quickly and successfully it adapts itself depends largely on the attitude of the majority of the parliamentary party. It cannot be a matter of pride for any constituency to have a Member who impedes this process of change, and expresses nothing but regret for what has gone and suspicion of what is coming. The die-hards are as important to a party as a brake is to a motor-car, but a Member of Parliament should be judged by how much he contributes, not by how much he resists. His loyalty should be measured by his fidelity to his party's ultimate aims, not by the degree of his day-to-day obedience. It is of little importance if from time to time he is out of step; what matters is whether he is out of direction; and whether his pace is too quick or too slow to keep him in constant sight of the main body.

A Member need not always reflect the opinions of the inner group of his Association. The orthodoxy of his views need not increase in proportion to the size of his majority. It is constituencies like Bournemouth, above all, which should be able to afford the luxury of occasional dissent. In the marginal seats, the Member must carefully guard against the loss of a single vote. The great majority of Bournemouth Conservatives would rightly resent any suggestion that, because they have given their Member a safe seat, they require of him strict compliance with their views.

It is only if he consistently defies them and the party, that he would ultimately forfeit all their confidence.

Have I consistently defied them? According to my division record, I have not. I have voted in 1170 divisions out of a possible 1344 since I became their Member of Parliament.[1] On every occasion except two I have voted in the Government lobby. Once (Suez) I abstained; and once, on a minor amendment to the Local Government Bill which seriously affected Bournemouth's interests as a seaside resort, I voted against the Government. The capital punishment divisions were free votes. This is not a heavily loaded charge-sheet. I do not believe that on reflection most Conservatives would maintain that my conduct in Parliament over the years amounts to an attitude of defiance or revolt.

But, it may be said, my attitude in the constituency has been unsatisfactory. In the minds of those who think themselves committed by the action which they took against me eighteen months ago, it may appear so. Having taken that action, it is only natural that they should now think up every reason for justifying it. But let them recollect the atmosphere of our last General Election. All my alleged errors, except Suez, were made before that date, and yet there was no moment when our partnership was more cordial or more fruitful. On the periphery of the Association, among those 20,000 Conservatives who have never belonged to it, there is little resentment of the two occasions when I felt bound to differ from the party line. I am received everywhere in Bournemouth and Christchurch, except in the inner Conservative circle, with tolerance and, I think, respect. Many of the two towns' leading men and women have openly supported me. Why should some of the Association's members feel obliged to exhibit a hostility which is shared by almost nobody outside it, and by a bare majority within it?

Their verdict will be given on the eve of the next General Election. For the reasons which I explained towards the end of Chapter Two,[2] I do not intend to stand at the election as an Independent candidate, now that the Association has again opened its doors to all genuine applicants for membership. I only

---

[1] Figures supplied by Conservative Central Office up till May 13th, 1958.
[2] See pp. 59-60.

reminded my Executive of my constitutional right to do so, when it seemed that they were preparing to crush all independence of judgement within the Association itself. This is a Conservative dispute, and it must be settled by Conservatives. They must have the candidate and the Member whom they want. If, in making their final considered choice, they reject me for another, I will go without resentment.

Let no Conservatives say afterwards that they had no chance to support my candidature, because they did not join the Association in time to qualify for a vote within it. They must join now. The Association is far too small. Its membership has declined since the controversy started. There are nearly 30,000 Conservative voters in Bournemouth East and Christchurch. Only about 5,000 of them are today members of the Association. I have offered to accept the Executive's veto on any applicant for membership whose Conservatism is suspect. Every genuine Conservative has the right to join on payment of a minimum of 2/6 a year. If they do not join, they will have no voice at all in one of the most important decisions which the Association has ever had to make.

I have often suggested that the issue should be decided by a form of 'primary election', confined to members of the Association, and held soon after the election date is known. A meeting would be called in the largest hall available in Bournemouth. Admission would be by ticket, and every paid-up member would have the right to attend. Both Major Friend and I would have an equal chance to address the meeting. At the conclusion of our speeches, there would be a vote between us on a secret ballot. The simple majority would decide. If I were defeated, I would immediately accept my dismissal, and play no part in the election locally. If Major Friend were defeated, I hope that he would do the same. I still believe that this is the fairest and cleanest method. It was rejected by Major Grant as 'airy-fairy nonsense'.

But it will be impossible for the Executive to avoid giving Bournemouth Conservatives the right to choose the candidate and Member whom they prefer. There is another method. By law an adoption meeting must be held about three weeks before polling day, at the outset of the election campaign. Every person who has been a member of the Association for at least a month before the date of the meeting, will be entitled to attend it. Its purpose will be to adopt the official Conservative candidate. Even if only the name of Major Friend is put before the meeting, and if I am not admitted to the hall, those inside can vote for or against that one name. A vote against it will be equivalent to a vote for me. If the official nominee does not receive a majority, he cannot become the Conservative candidate, and it will then be open to any member of the audience to propose that I shall be adopted in his place. That proposal will be put to the vote, and if carried, I shall become the official Conservative candidate for the election.

In this way my Conservative constituents will be enabled finally and democratically to end this long controversy. To repeat the Prime Minister's words of advice, 'I am sure the Association in deciding its action, will bear in mind the best interests of the Conservative Party, nationally as well as locally.'

Chapter Seven

PEOPLE, PARLIAMENT AND PARTY

Burke's views on representation—Mr Amery's views—the public's views—the demand for leadership—the silent conflict between people and Parliament— fiction of party homogeneity—the benefits of party cohesion—the Member's four roles—his ultimate duty.

A CENTURY and more ago, a politician would quite bluntly tell the people that they were not to be trusted. Walter Bagehot considered that 'constituency government is the precise opposite of parliamentary government. It is the government of immoderate persons far from the scene of action, instead of the government of moderate persons close to the scene of action.' This language was but a slight toning down of the views which Burke had expressed a hundred years earlier: 'The opinion of the merely vulgar is a miserable rule even with regard to themselves, on account of their violence and instability.' Burke was only a democrat in the sense that he believed in government *for* the people. The governors were to be drawn from the territorial aristocracy, which alone had the necessary education and detachment to govern sensibly. 'We are enlarged in our opinions,' he once told the House of Commons, 'while the people are confined.'

What purpose, then, did he see in holding elections, limited though the franchise was? If the people were so stupid that a representative was doing them a service by ignoring their views, why were any of them permitted to choose their representatives, whom they might choose so wrongly? It was for this reason that Burke approved the system of rotten and pocket boroughs, and after his rejection by Bristol, sat for one of them without a qualm. He considered the idea of extending the franchise as abhorrent, both on the grounds that the people had no education, and because government would become impossible if everybody had a share in it, however indirect:

'By this unprincipled facility of changing the State as often, as much, and in as many ways, as there are floating fancies and fashions,' he wrote, 'the whole chain and continuity of the commonwealth would be broken. No one generation could link with the other. Men would become little better than the flies of the summer.'[1]

His defence of the American colonists was not based on abstract justice, but on national self-interest: 'the question with me is not whether you have a right to render your people miserable, but whether it is not in your interest to make them happy.' His hatred of the French revolutionaries was founded on contempt for mob rule, which he feared might spread to England. When he quarrelled with Bristol, it was not because of any abstract theory of parliamentary supremacy, but because he considered his constituents prejudiced and obtuse. Burke's opinions on the relations between a Member and his constituents are regularly quoted today because they are statements of abiding political truth. But they were uttered in a wholly different context. We have rejected his theory of oligarchy, and proved that his fears of universal suffrage were totally misconceived. It is all the more remarkable that his central message to Parliament has stood the test of time.

The difference between Burke's views on democracy and our own is illustrated by Leo Amery's definition of our system as 'democracy by consent and not by delegation, government of the people, for the people, with but not by the people.'[2] Even that definition, with which I wholly agree, might now be considered by some as already outdated, since it still contains a trace of Burke's oligarchic attitude, namely, that Parliament knows best, and is to some extent detached from the people whom it serves. In Burke's time only men like Burke had a theory of representation. Now the people have one too. It is not quite the same as Leo Amery's. The vote, they say, is not a latch-key given on trust to every person when he reaches the age of 21, but a power which the people would ultimately have seized, even in England, if it had been withheld from them much longer. They demand the right to interfere in government, the right to be wrong, the right to suffer the consequences of their own prejudices. They will not be treated as children or incompetents. They employ a Member of Parliament as they would employ a plumber or a piano-tuner, to do a job. His job is representation. That does not mean that he

[1] Edmund Burke, *Reflections on the Revolution in France.*
[2] In *Parliament. A Survey.* ed. Lord Campion, London, 1952.

is to be controlled at every stage of his work by their instructions, any more than is the plumber or piano-tuner. But it does mean that he must pay attention to their wishes. They will not be fobbed off with the alternative theory that true representation sometimes means doing the opposite of what they ask.

The argument would be reasonable if only the people could be as precise in their instructions to their representatives as they are to their plumber when they ask him to mend a leak, or to their piano-tuner when they ask him to make the piano fit to play. In politics such precision is clearly impossible. So a false precision is substituted for a real one by telling the representative to follow the party-line. This is a development quite unforeseeable by Burke. The people have not abused their power in the way which he foresaw, by demanding the impossible and continuously wavering in their opinions according to their 'floating fancies and fashions'. Their opinions are stable to a fault, and their demands are for obedience to the party more than to themselves. They have handed back to the parties the power which they wrested from Parliament.

In previous chapters I have illustrated this tendency by two different instances. The controversy over capital punishment was an example of party pressure to reverse a policy which the party's leaders considered wrong. Suez was an example of even stronger pressure to sustain a policy which the party's leaders considered right. In both instances party opinion did not form the policy: it was formed by it. If the Home Secretary had emphatically declared that abolition of the death sentence for an experimental period of five years was a risk worth taking in view of the experience of foreign countries, or if the Prime Minister had said from the start that Nasser could better be punished by economic than by military sanctions, who can doubt that their lead would have been followed and acclaimed? The electors hold the ultimate power by their votes, but they tend to distrust their own judgement. They instinctively respond to leadership, and give every benefit of the doubt to their party-leader when his policy apparently goes astray. They expect their representatives to adopt the same attitude. Parliament is less merciful to the leaders, but more charitable to their dissentient followers. The shifts of reputation among political leaders are caused by the parliamentary parties, not by the national party organizations, which simply reflect, after a time-lag, the views of Westminster. And while political loyalty is a major virtue in the country, it is more a matter of convenience than of ethics in the House.

The different attitude to party is, I believe, at the root of the silent conflict between people and Parliament. It has been largely caused by Parliament itself. Parliament has created a false image of itself. In their efforts to retain their voting strength in the country, the two major parties have let it be imagined that loyalty is more important to them than judgement, and that a split in the party is the greatest of all disasters. The party-leaders have not followed this rule in their own careers, and they do not expect their parliamentary colleagues to follow it. But the party-battle, which is at least half a pretence in Parliament, has become a grim reality outside. It is seldom openly admitted, particularly by Conservatives, that the difference of attitude between the two wings of each major party is at least as important as the differences between the two parties themselves. The character of a Government or Opposition is determined by this continuing internal party debate, but it is barely recognized that such a debate is consistent with the party's survival.

Every shade in the British political spectrum can be found between the right-wing Conservative and the left-wing Socialist. The Fascist and Communist movements are so insignificant that neither are represented in Parliament at all: one is ultra-violet and the other ultra-red. The visible spectrum is snipped in half at a convenient point, and the two halves are laid out along opposite benches in the House of Commons. It is quite wrong to imagine that there is an intermediate range of colours unrepresented in either major party. It is only the delusion that all Conservatives fall within a narrow range of blues, and all Socialists within a narrow range of reds, which has given the Liberal Party the opportunity to gather support from the intervening greens and yellows. So the fiction of party homogeneity is a tactical disadvantage to Conservative and Socialists, as well as a parliamentary monstrosity.

It is not as if the parties were divided from each other by

6*

differences of principle as basic as they pretend. Macaulay aptly compared the Whigs and Tories to the fore and hind legs of a running stag. It is still true of Socialists and Conservatives. Their most important principles are British principles, common to both of them. For example, freedom of speech, equality under the law, Christianity, the Crown, the right to privacy, the right of a man to make the most of his talents, importance of the family, international morality, respect for the interests of minorities and colonial peoples—all of them principles strenuously denied by contemporary European and Asiatic dictatorships. There is certainly a difference in the interpretation given to them by the two parties, but even this distinction has become blurred. A Conservative Government can support a national air-line, to the great disadvantage of the independent operator, whose right to free competition would have been unchallenged ten years ago. A leading Socialist like Mr Shinwell can approve of the Suez action, when it might have been supposed that every tenet of his party would have been outraged by it. And who could say that there is now a profound difference in the approach of the two parties to such previously explosive subjects as opportunity and initiative, the duty of the strong to help the weak, Communism in the Trades Unions, or the cure for unemployment? Perhaps the only serious disagreements are on the question of unearned or half-earned incomes and the degree of state interference in private industry. They are important differences, and the most is made of them by both sides, because for a politician to lack a dispute is as terrible as for an actor to lack a script.

It is not so much principles which divide the two parties, as attitudes, which are themselves the product of constant party warfare. Each side presents to the public the most unflattering portrait of their opponents that they can devise. Such great clouds of smoke are generated that it is assumed that at least a small fire must lurk beneath. When Conservatives are called the upholders of privilege, or Socialists are said to be little different in essentials from Communists, though neither accusation is true, in the course of years a colour-wash spreads over their parties which they find impossible to remove. Their chief method of defence is to deepen the colour with which they have successfully daubed their opponents. The leaders of the opposite party are identified with the most extreme opinions of their followers, and their changes of heart and mind are represented as vacillation or humbug. It is constantly emphasized that if the electorate is misguided enough to return them to power, their whole attitude to our common problems will be impregnated by prejudices beyond their control.

In this way, the parties magnify their differences of outlook. If the purpose is to present the public at the election with a clearcut choice, to that extent the fiction is harmless and even useful. A man cannot vote for a spectrum: he can only vote for a colour. The deceit actually clarifies his mind. Nothing would be gained at election-time if candidates of the same party were to put forward completely contradictory policies, or candidates of different parties indistinguishable policies. If after the election, a party were seen to be constantly quarrelling among themselves, the impression would grow that if they cannot govern themselves, they are not fit to be entrusted with the government of the country. 'The British people,' Herbert Morrison has said, 'rightly attach importance to a party being sufficiently coherent and united to give the country a Government not only of sound policy but of adequate strength and unity of purpose.'[1] With all this I agree. But there is all the difference between anarchy and freedom of discussion. A party's unity is not incompatible with honest dissent. Let us recognize in the country as well as in Parliament that the system is at least partly based on a fiction; that when serious disagreement arises, it should not be crushed but absorbed; that a party, like a committee, should evolve its policies by interpenetration of differences, not all of which need be concealed behind closed doors; and that it is no more shameful for a party to borrow ideas from its opponents than it is for an army to make use of a captured supply-train.

Parliament implicitly recognizes these distinctions, particularly the Conservative parliamentary party. In the constituencies they are more confused, because there is a double relationship involved, between the Member and his party, and the Member and his electors. No firm rules can be laid down to govern this relation-

---

[1] Herbert Morrison, *Government and Parliament*. Oxford, 1954.

ship, but there are certain considerations which should always affect it.

In normal circumstances, the Member represents his constituency in the sense that he has a duty to bring its grievances to the attention of Parliament, except when they appear to him to be wholly unreasonable, and to seek opportunities to help his constituents, even before they approach him for help. At the same time he must try to fuse his constituents' interests with the national interest, to avoid turning Parliament into a congress of conflicting local or sectional claims. He is not a barrister pleading on behalf of a client, but a member of a Council anxious to reach the fairest compromise, with a watching brief for a particular part of the population, whose problems may not be exactly paralleled anywhere else and are therefore of importance to the Council as a whole.

Secondly, the Member is one of a large body chosen to represent the nation. He is chosen because it is assumed that he has, or will soon acquire, a special aptitude for absorbing information and reaching sensible conclusions based on what he reads and hears. Parliament is collectively a cross-section of the nation, but in a different sense from the first 630 men and women to emerge after 8.30 a.m. from the Oxford Circus tube-station, because it is trained in controversy, and they are not. It expresses every shade of opinion in the country, but its debates are not kaleidoscopic; they take the form of a discussion more than of a series of orations, and 'the sense of the House' is often recognizable after no more than half an hour. As far as it will ever be possible for a few hundred people to sum up the feelings of many millions, the House of Commons achieves it, but this will only continue to happen if the individual Member considers his national responsibility to be greater even than his constituency responsibility.

Thirdly, the Member belongs to a parliamentary party. He owes it allegiance, but it is not the same as military allegiance. He has not bound himself to follow it blindly wherever its leaders may take him. He must give them the benefit of doubt, but when his disagreement is absolute, he must express it, privately at first, but publicly if he has failed to influence them or deter them, and if his own convictions remain unshaken. Naturally the form of his protest will vary from a mildly remonstrative speech to an out-right vote in the opposition lobby. It will depend on the strength of his feeling, the amount of support he has for it in Parliament and in the country, the importance of the subject, the damage his protest will do to the party, whether his party forms the Government or is in opposition to it, the size of the Government's majority, and even the stage which the Parliament has reached in its life. But the principle is clear: a Member would be failing in his duty even to those of his friends whom he most bitterly attacks, if on those rare occasions he lacks the moral courage to say what he thinks right.

Finally, the Member has his obligations to the party-workers in his constituency. They are the most important group of his con-stituents, but their wishes and interests should not be allowed to dominate all others. He must consult them regularly, and where there is initial disagreement, try to win them round to his point-of-view. Where he holds no strong opinions on a subject, he should follow their lead as far as it is ascertainable. When he disagrees, he owes them not only a full explanation, but a deeper study of the problem than they can possibly make of it. If it is a question of conscience, he should weigh up, among all the other moral factors involved in his decision, the amount of distress which his disagreement will cause to them. He should make very clear to them the distinction between disagreement and defiance, which many of them would otherwise be tempted to identify, and explain that he has neither ignored nor betrayed them in differing from them.

As the moment approaches for an irrevocable decision, he should review once again all the considerations that have led to their disagreement, and not be too proud to suggest a compromise. But in the last resort his decision is his own, and he must not shirk it, whatever the distress it causes to others, whatever the damage to himself.

APPENDIX

Speech to the Conservative Association of Bournemouth East
and Christchurch
at the Selwyn Hall, Boscombe, Bournemouth, December 5th 1956
by NIGEL NICOLSON, MP[1]

I AM PROFOUNDLY sorry that I should have caused distress to
so many of you who have done much for the Conservative Party,
and with whom I have had such a long and happy personal
relationship. But I have not come here to plead for your forgive-
ness; I have come to ask for your understanding. I still think that
I was right to do what I did. Everything that has happened since
our intervention in Egypt has confirmed my original belief that it
was wrong in principle and needlessly dangerous in practice. I
think that it has not succeeded for reasons which were predictable
but which were ignored, and because we overestimated our
ability to defy the rest of the world.

Let me first explain to you why I thought as I did, and then
come to the point on which the Resolutions have concentrated—
why I said what I thought.

From the start of the Suez crisis I believed that any attempt by
the French and British to solve it by force would cause more
trouble than it would cure. This was not because I was opposed to
the use of force under any circumstances, particularly against a
petty dictator like Nasser; nor because I thought that this and
other problems could safely be left to the United Nations. I did
not. But it seemed to me and many others that there were better
ways of dealing with Nasser—better in the sense that they would
be more effective, less costly, and above all, that they would
command the support of the whole British nation and all our
Allies.

I won't go over the arguments again. Briefly it was the method
of combining the immediate use of economic sanctions to prove
to Nasser that his type of highway robbery does not pay, with the
threat of military sanctions to block his future ambitions. This idea
was not of course my own; it was suggested during the summer

---

[1] For the circumstances in which this speech was made, see p. 148.

by several eminent Conservatives. It seemed to me sensible. The alternative, the use of force by us and the French, appeared full of risks to our alliances, our Commonwealth, our oil supplies, our oil-routes, our economy and our reputation, and we knew in advance that the Labour and Liberal Parties in Parliament would not support it. Many people in our party thought these risks unnecessarily great, when there were better methods open to us to achieve our object. I thought so too, and I still think so.

I put forward these ideas in a series of speeches which I made in different parts of the constituency in late September and early October. It was always the same speech, because I wanted to test your reactions very carefully. Many of you here must have heard it. I made it first to the Queen's Park Ladies Branch on September 20th. The same evening I repeated it in Christchurch to an audience of business and professional women. I made it publicly on September 26th at the Quality Inn, Jumpers, when it was fully reported in the local Press. On October 2nd I was at St Andrew's, Boscombe, on the 3rd at Strouden Park, on the 8th with the Boscombe East Young Conservatives, and on the 9th at the Immanuel Hall, Southbourne. Again and again I argued these same ideas and invited your comments. The reaction was almost unanimous at each of the meetings—that the use of military force to solve the Suez Canal crisis, unless Nasser went further than he had already gone, would be unwise and unnecessary.

Nasser did not go further than he had already gone. In a way I wish he had. If he had attacked Israel or stopped our ships, for example, nobody would have objected if we had invaded Egypt and occupied the Canal Zone. But he didn't attack Israel. Israel attacked him, and for the first time in his life, Nasser appeared in the eyes of the rest of the world to have some sort of legitimate grievance, however much he had provoked Israel in the past. When we and France, in effect, joined in on Israel's side, he had a double grievance, and Russia and America were forced into an unnatural alliance to stop us.

We were quite right to intervene to stop the war from spreading—indeed we were bound by treaty to do so. But I think we were wrong to intervene in such a way as to cause our Allies and the Commonwealth to think that we were seizing on the pretext of the Israeli attack to settle our old quarrel with Nasser about the Canal. The two problems were distinct.

I believe that as soon as the attack started, we should have invoked the Tripartite Declaration. This famous Declaration was made in 1950 by the United States, France and ourselves. By it, we all promised to intervene to stop any war which broke out between Jew and Arab. President Eisenhower at once declared on October 30th that the United States would act in accordance with this Treaty, but Britain and France had by that time already declared it to be a dead letter, without even telling the Americans or the Commonwealth that we were going to do so. I think that all our subsequent troubles arose from this mistake. If we had invoked the Treaty, landed our main force between the two combatants at Gaza instead of behind one of them at Port Said, bombed the Israeli airfields and armoured formations as well as the Egyptian, and then referred our action afterwards to the United Nations, we would have stopped the war more quickly, and nobody except the Communists would have questioned our good faith.

This is the core of my objection. It is not a matter of tactics. It is a matter of principle. For years we have been saying that the Tripartite Declaration and the Baghdad Pact were the twin pillars of our policy in the Middle East. At a single blow we destroyed one and gravely endangered the other. For years we have been careful (over-careful, I would say) not to let our friendship towards Israel trespass too far on our friendship for the Arabs. Now every Arab is convinced that Britain has deliberately helped the Jews at the moment when the Jews attacked an Arab country. Almost the whole world now believes that our main motive was to reoccupy the Canal under cover of the Israeli attack. Some go so far as to say that we knew about it in advance. It is sad, I think, that we should ever have made it possible for our allies to level such charges against a British Government, but there is no doubt that they are believed by millions and millions of people who were once our friends and who now distrust us. This has done our country tremendous harm. Even if the United Nations had not existed, it would have made little difference. The world would have condemned us just the same.

Let me make it very clear what I think about the United Nations. Few people, and I am not one of them, seriously imagine that it is physically strong enough to prevent Governments doing almost anything they want. It could not stop the Russians murdering the Hungarians, and it would not by itself have solved either the Canal problem or the Palestine problem. I think it may have been given a job too big for it in the Canal Zone at this moment. I have always totally disagreed with the Labour Party (whose belief in the United Nations has often been absurdly idealistic) that the Security Council should have been allowed to tell us what to do on October 30th. It was the responsibility of the Western Powers to decide which action to take. But if we were to be true to our own party's often-declared belief that the United Nations is the foundation on which we should base our hopes for the future of the world, we should not have acted outside the spirit and letter of its Charter, when we could have acted just as effectively (indeed, more so) within it. In our last election manifesto, we used these words: 'We are determined to keep our western alliance defensive in character, and to indulge in no provocation.' That is what I mean by the 'spirit of the Charter'. That was the argument which I constantly put forward in your name and in the party's name at the General Election. I reminded our electors in Bournemouth and Christchurch that when we created the United Nations, we undertook never to use force against a foreign power unless we or one of our Allies were attacked, or in execution of a published treaty. Russia has several times broken that pledge, I said, but a British Conservative Government never will. Was I wrong to have said that eighteen months ago? Am I wrong to remind you of it now?

I am not arguing on the basis of a Sunday-school morality, ignoring the fact that Nasser is an evil and ruthless man. I am much more concerned with the practical consequences of our having antagonized the world. Of course we shall recover in time most of our moral credit, just as we shall eventually recover from the blow to our economy. But in future it will be just that bit more difficult for British representatives to persuade the foreigner to accept our point of view. Contracts will go to others, and Governments will be more wary of our promises and have less confidence in our judgement. Particularly is that so of the Americans, who grudgingly took our advice over Indo-China and Formosa and worked closely with us at both Geneva Conferences, only to find that we have acted in Egypt without telling them, because (so they believe), we knew that they would object if we did tell them. Imagine what we would have felt, if within a week of a General Election, the United States had launched an attack on Indo-China without even informing us beforehand. We would have been extremely angry. Well, the anger of the Americans at what we have done in Egypt may have led them in these last few weeks to exaggerated protests, but they will not be impressed by shouts of recrimination from Britain. Whatever we say, we shall remain the guilty party in their eyes. They feel deeply that we and the French have done them wrong, and recklessly weakened the Atlantic Alliance. What people feel today dictates how they will act tomorrow.

To sum up, then, these are some of the reasons why I felt that our attack on Egypt was a great mistake. If our object was to stop a small war developing into a big war, the machinery of the Tripartite Declaration was there for exactly that purpose. If we wished to settle the Canal problem, it could have been better settled by economic than by military means. If we wished to counter a Communist threat in the Middle East we should have informed the Americans and the Commonwealth, who would have helped us to win or buy the friendship of the non-Egyptian Arabs and to strengthen our existing alliances in the area; instead, by acting alone outside the letter of the law, we have presented the Communists with a terrible propaganda weapon, and an opportunity, as the last few days have shown, to penetrate more deeply into Syria and elsewhere. If we intended to crush Nasser, we have only succeeded in enabling him to cover up his humiliating defeat by Israel, and to pose as a hero and martyr. If we feared for the safety of our shipping and citizens in Egypt, the Canal would not have been blocked nor our people expelled if we had intervened against both sides near Egypt's eastern frontier instead of against Egypt alone on the Canal itself. All these risks inherent in the operation were foreseeable, and I think they should have been foreseen in time to prevent us from embarking upon it.

Feeling as strongly as I did that Britain had done herself an injustice and a great harm, I had to make up my mind whether to deceive you into thinking that I was fully in support of the Government's action. I decided that I could not and should not, once the fighting was over. How could I have answered those hundreds of letters which I was receiving from Conservatives who were as shocked as I was, assuring them that I had changed my mind and that I now totally disagreed with their views? How could I hope to have any influence on future events, if I gave support to a policy which (as so many of you knew because I had consulted you) I had always felt to be profoundly wrong?

For eight days, however, I said nothing publicly in criticism of our action, while I kept the party Whips, the chairman of our Association, and a few others, constantly informed of my real feelings. I was waiting until the troops had stopped fighting. Then, on November 7th, the day after the cease-fire, I took advantage of an invitation from the Bournemouth branch of the United Nations Association to tell the truth. I made my statement at a moment when my protest would do least harm to the Government and most harm to myself. I notified our agent of my intention. It was a public meeting, and several of you were able to be present. It took place less than a mile away from this hall.

Looking back, that still seems to me the right moment to have chosen for my protest. It could not have been delayed indefinitely. If I had come to you in 1958 and told you that I had been lying to you for two years about the events of November 1956, I don't think you would have thought much of my honesty or political courage. Besides, it was very much in the minds of the moderate group in the party that unless some of us made our influence felt and our voices heard in the early stages, we would be powerless to help the Government resist the extremists when the moment for more moderate policies came. That moment has come now. If, during these past few weeks, the voice of the Conservative Party had been exclusively the voice of the Suez Group in Parliament, our country would have been committed by this time to a course of action which would be almost beyond repair. Sir Anthony Eden was absolutely right to stop when he did, and he was able to stop because he knew that he had his supporters. If, as many people advocated, we had continued to fight our way from Port Said to Suez, after the Jews and Egyptians had ceased fire, we should not be in a stronger bargaining position now, but in a far weaker one, because Nasser would have attracted even more support from the rest of the world. It might even have started a Third World War, with this country and the western Alliance divided, or caused our financial ruin. For the same reasons, we are right to withdraw now. The continued presence of our troops at Port Said can do no more good than a splinter in a thumb—it simply increases the area of inflammation. This is the Government's argument, and I wholly support it. It will not be I, but others, who will hesitate before voting in the Government lobby tomorrow night.[1]

I believe that many of you do not condemn me for what I did, because you do not consider it to be a Member of Parliament's highest duty to do what he is told by his party, or even by yourselves. In all normal circumstances, a Member should certainly stay with his party, and not allow minor disagreements to upset its unity. As you know, I have never claimed complete freedom of judgement for myself, and I have bowed to your wishes, even when the Government has left a decision to a free vote of the House. Most of my Conservative friends now tell me I was wrong to have done that. I do not think I was.

But the attack on Egypt was something quite different from capital punishment. It took us all by surprise. It was a major act of policy. Members of Parliament had information about it which could not be publicly revealed. We had to make up our own minds, and at once. That is what Parliament is for. Just because it did involve the armed forces and our national honour, Parliament was obliged to scrutinize it all the more closely. Such scrutiny is not the exclusive business of the Opposition.

I do not think that there is a single one of us who did not have some misgivings when we first heard of our ultimatum to Israel and Egypt. But sooner or later we all had to come down on one side or the other, and the divisions that soon arose in the country simply reflected the divisions which had originally been in all our

[1] On the motion to withdraw our forces from Egypt. Fifteen Conservative Members abstained.

minds. Paradoxically, this was not really a party matter at all. Up and down the country, Socialists found themselves backing Sir Anthony and Conservatives opposing him. The Church was divided, the lawyers, the soldiers, the scholars, the doctors, the Trades Unions, the Press. It is not enough to dismiss as foolish the opinions of responsible men—I am not talking of the Opposition—who disagreed with the Government, to say that papers like *The Times* and the *Spectator* have 'gone Socialist', that the Archbishop of Canterbury is no judge of the morality of an action, or that men like Colonel Hasler, the leader of the cockleshell heroes, and thousands and thousands of loyal Conservatives throughout the United Kingdom, are all traitors. Why, these noble words 'loyalty', 'courage', 'patriotism' and others, will soon have lost all their meaning if they are to be used to suffocate all honest self-criticism. Half a nation cannot be impeached for treachery by the other half. Indeed it would only have been shameful if not a single Conservative could have been found in Parliament to express the deep resentment felt by so many outside.

Not one of us on the back benches or in the Government who openly or privately criticized our attack on Egypt, was made to feel by the party leaders that he had done something discreditable. The Prime Minister had made a tremendously bold decision, which he sustained, until exhaustion overcame him, with wonderful calm and fortitude. Never by a word or a look did he or his fellow Cabinet Ministers seek to condemn us, and I do not believe that he did so in his heart. He knew the risks of this operation, and one which he certainly foresaw, because he had seen the warning signals when Parliament was recalled in September, was that his action could not be supported by every Member on his own side. If he had been as shocked by our opposition as some of our constituents were, he would certainly have imposed the penalty devised for exactly this type of situation. He would have withdrawn the whip. He has not withdrawn it from any one of us. Does that not imply that he attributed our opposition to conscientious and legitimate disagreement? Should you not do the same?

That, after all, is the tradition of our party. It is the boast of Conservatives that we allow each other freedom of speech. We are trusted not to differ from the accepted policy for reasons of self-interest, or in ignorance of the facts, or on a sudden whim. Of course, if any Member suddenly finds himself unable to accept one of the party's basic principles, there is no longer any room for him in the party. But that is not the case here. We have not opposed a principle. On the contrary, we are protesting that a principle has been broken.

May I remind you of the words used by a great Conservative statesman at another crisis of this kind:

'No man,' he said, 'would willingly sever the links which bind him with colleagues and friends. . . . But there are occasions when strong political convictions must override all other considerations. Of such occasions only the individual himself can be the judge.'[1]

Those were the opening words of Sir Anthony Eden's speech when he resigned as Foreign Secretary in February 1938. He too found himself unable to support his Prime Minister at a critical moment of our affairs. Six months later we had Munich, and a great revolt against the Government, in which Sir Winston himself took part. In May 1940, on the very day when Hitler opened his attack on the allied line, the Prime Minister resigned because thirty-three Conservatives voted with the Opposition on a motion of censure. Among them were men like Leo Amery, Duff Cooper, the present Lord Hailsham, and Harold Macmillan. Who would condemn them now, though at the time they all acted against the wishes of the Cabinet and a great majority of their constituents? They were not asked to resign their seats. I think that we should carefully ponder these parallels before committing the party to a different precedent tonight.

I am sure that each one of you has at different times complained that Members of Parliament are becoming increasingly submissive, and that the merits of a situation or policy are too often clouded by purely party quarrels. I therefore ask you not to crush them when on occasions, even against your own wishes, they dare to show their independence of judgement and depth of personal conviction. A party from which all extremities are severed is a lifeless trunk. In your hearts, you want a Parliament of

[1] *Hansard,* vol. 332, col. 45. February 21st, 1938.

independent men, and you want as your own representative a man
who believes passionately in our party's principles, but is not
afraid to speak his mind when he sincerely considers that one of
them has been violated. This is what the greatest of all parliamentarians, Sir Winston Churchill, had to say on this subject:

What is the use of sending Members to the House of Commons who
say just the popular things of the moment and merely endeavour to
give satisfaction to the Government Whips by cheering loudly every
Ministerial platitude and by walking through the lobbies oblivious
of the criticisms they hear? People talk about our parliamentary in-
stitutions and parliamentary democracy, but if these are to survive, it
will not be because the constituencies return tame, docile, subservient
Members and try to stamp out every form of independent judgement.

In this constituency lives one of Sir Winston's oldest and most
intimate friends. He is my most eminent constituent. He is also
President of our Association. Lord Quickswood. Two days ago,
he wrote an open letter to a friend, and I have the permission of
both of them to quote from it tonight. This is what he says:

The question has of course been a thousand times discussed, but I
think it is safe to say that no Member of Parliament should ever be
required to retire from Parliament on the grounds that he is against
his party. He can of course, in effect, be excluded from Parliament by
the method of running a candidate against him from the ranks of his
own supporters: that has happened to me and it has happened to a
great many people, and we were defeated by the return of a party
opponent who had a majority over our supporters' divided forces. But
this is a matter for the next Election. While a man is in Parliament, he
cannot be turned out of Parliament except by a vote of the House of
Commons, who can expel him as unworthy to be a Member of
Parliament.

This, however, is not the present purpose, as no one complains of
Mr Nicolson's personal fitness for Parliament. The complaint seems to
be that he has voted according to his conscience but against his party,
and I have no hesitation whatever in saying that he has done quite
rightly in thus voting. He was sent to Parliament to be a representative
of the whole Commons of the Realm speaking in the name of the whole
Commons, and not as a delegate of the particular constituency who had
the right to appoint him. He was appointed by them as being, in their
judgement, a good representative of the whole body of the Commons.

Being so appointed, it is his business to use the best of his conscience and abilities to serve in the House of Commons by expressing his opinion according to his conscience. He is therefore entirely free from blame for abstaining from voting for his party on a particular occasion when his conscience directed him to do so.

I remain, yours sincerely,

Quickswood

On advocacy of that quality, any man would be glad to let his fate depend. And it is for those reasons, with which I believe you will one day all agree, even if some of you do not agree now, that I must decline any invitation to resign my seat.

INDEX